Succe
from Around the World

In Budapest, Hungary, a student wanted to learn English quickly enough to win a BBC contest. Using the sleep-learning method, he memorized one thousand and twenty-six English words in six weeks and won first prize!

In Minnesota, several hundred people stopped smoking when they tuned their radios to an overnight sleep-learning program designed to help them quit.

In England, a television producer announced that he would learn Spanish by the sleep-learning method. After two weeks, he demonstrated his success by broadcasting in Spanish—with a very good accent!

In California, 70 people a day reported that listening to an early morning radio broadcast of sleep-learning messages dramatically decreased their desire to overeat.

LEARN WHILE YOU SLEEP

JAMES P. DUFFY

AVON BOOKS ▲ NEW YORK

LEARN WHILE YOU SLEEP is an original publication of Avon Books. This work has never before appeared in book form.

AVON BOOKS
A division of
The Hearst Corporation
1350 Avenue of the Americas
New York, New York 10019

First Avon Books Printing: July 1991

AVON TRADEMARK REG. U.S. PAT. OFF. AND IN OTHER COUNTRIES, MARCA REGISTRADA, HECHO EN U.S.A.

Printed in the U.S.A.

RA 10 9 8 7 6 5 4 3 2 1

To
PAT

Acknowledgments

So many people contributed to the researching and writing of this book that it is almost impossible to mention them all. There are a few who, by their efforts or ideas, were of such help that they should be singled out here.

My close friend Vince Ricci made a major contribution to the entire book and deserves my deepest appreciation, as does my wife, Kathleen, whose enthusiastic support and tireless efforts were cheerfully given over the many years of the book's incubation. Claire Wolf and John Douglas made so many excellent recommendations to the original manuscript that they deserve a special thanks.

Dr. Ernst Schmidhofer read and commented on the validity of much of the scientific information used. Mr. Geoffrey Stocker also read and contributed to the early drafts of the manuscript. To both men I once again extend my grateful appreciation.

Contents

Foreword Geoffrey Stocker, President
British Research Centre for the
Development of Hypnopaedic
Learning 1

A Note to the Reader 9

1. **Unlocking Your Mind**
   Facts and Fictions 11
   The History of Sleep Learning 15
   Defining Sleep Learning 22

2. **The Power of Your Subconscious**
   Your Subconscious at Work 26
   The Center of Creativity 35
   Subconscious Learning 39

3. **How We Learn and Remember**
   The Conditions for Learning 44
   How We Remember 48

Repeating to Remember 52

Remembering and Forgetting 55

Learning, Memory, and Sleep 58

4.   The Mysterious Third of Our Lives

What Sleep Is 62

Why We Can't Live Without Sleep 68

Dreams and Their Function 71

The Importance of Dreams...................... 76

The Laboratory Affect and Sleep Learning 78

Hypnosis, Sleep, and Learning 82

5.   How Sleep Learning Works

The Foundation of Sleep Learning 85

Listening While We Sleep 87

Reacting to What We Hear 92

Learning While Asleep 93

Relaxation Learning 100

Sleep Learning Around the World..............105

Sleep Learning Over the Radio 112

6.   Sleep Learning a Foreign Language

How Languages Are Taught 117

The Ladies Learn German......................120

A Course in Persian 123

Language Learning in the United States 124

7.   Sleep Learning as Therapy

Sleep Learning as Therapy 131

Breaking Bad Habits............................134

Helping a Stroke Victim........................136

Teaching Brain Damaged Children.............138

Cerebral Training 144

8. Sleep Learning and You

Becoming a Sleep Learner 146

Preparing Yourself for Sleep Learning 149

Do You Really Want to Learn? 152

Selecting What You Want to Learn 154

Relaxation Methods 156

9. How to Learn While You Sleep

Selecting the Right Equipment 164

How to Record Your Own Lessons 168

Using Prerecorded Tapes 170

Timing Lessons for Best Results 171

When and How to Use a Conditioning Tape ..172

10. Using Sleep Learning Lessons

To Learn a Foreign Language 177

To Break Bad Habits 181

For Weight Reduction 182

To Stop Smoking 186

To Build Self-Confidence 187

11. Answers to Commonly Asked Questions About Sleep Learning 189

Some Final Words 194

Appendix: Hypnopaedic Course in German 195

Foreword

by Geoffrey Stocker, President
British Research Centre for the
Development of Hypnopaedic Learning

I felt honored when Mr. Duffy invited me to write a Foreword to his book on sleep learning and soon became fully absorbed in reading it.

The book has been extremely well researched and the author has succeeded in bringing the whole subject up-to-date in a very illuminating manner. He writes with authority and conviction, revealing his wide knowledge of the subject based undoubtedly on his keen and inquiring mind.

My own interest in sleep learning started in 1960 while I was working in private practice as a hypnotherapist in London. I taught many of my patients to use self-hypnosis to accelerate their progress, and occasionally provided them with a personal tape during therapy to supplement treatment. I gradually realized that the recorded tapes, used in conjunction with basic treatment, were playing their own important part, undoubtedly because the subjects were already conditioned to be more receptive.

As a student, I frequently memorized lessons with

greater ease when studying in bed and finally dozing off than I did sitting at a table. Later, when taking a course in Speech at one of the London Academies, I recorded my part in a play on tape and played it back at night while falling asleep, only occasionally glancing at the script during the day. At rehearsals I was often surprised at the ease of recall. On another occasion, I learned a poem entirely by sleep learning, seeing the printed words only once—at the time of recording it. I still remember that poem! I did not arrive at any conclusions at that time, but discussed these experiences with friends and colleagues. Many had had similar experiences.

In 1962 the Sleep Learning Association was founded by a group of us, keen professionals in various fields: a journalist, a linguist, a social scientist, a psychologist. Later we gained the support and encouragement of the eminent psychiatrist Dr. M. N. Pai, MB, BS, DPM, MRCP, FRSM.

Through the various embassies in London we ferreted out what was going on elsewhere in the world, and soon discovered that the Russians had made great advances in sleep learning and were leading the way.

It was not an easy matter to communicate with scientists in Russia at that time, but gradually we did manage to start up correspondence with some, including A. M. Svyadoshch, V. N. Kulikov, and Professor L. A. Bliznitchenko. One of our team actually visited the U.S.S.R. to aid relations, and from then on a better exchange of information took place between our two countries. The support and encouragement we received from behind the Iron Curtain, as it was then known, was truly amazing. Of course much of the work going on was classified as secret and specific details of many experiments were unobtainable.

We learned that at a conference on Programmed Teaching held in Kiev in 1962, Bliznitchenko met Timofei

Rostunov, Head of the Kiev Higher Radio-Engineering School. As a result of that meeting, collaboration between the laboratory of experimental phonetics and the radio-engineering school took place, and the first organized experiments in group instruction during sleep were started. This was the year in which the Sleep Learning Association was founded.

We requested permission from Professor Bliznitchenko to translate one of his books into English and to publish it in Britain. He was delighted with the idea, and the book was published in 1967.

We translated other important articles and reports published in foreign journals into English and published them periodically in the *Quarterly Journal* of the Association to keep our members informed of all developments abroad.

In Great Britain we met a lot of opposition. The Ministry of Education showed no interest. The British Medical Association was unimpressed. And so we could only press ahead with our own research without any support whatsoever from the Establishment.

We occasionally suffered ridicule from the press: A report appeared in the *Sunday Press* of London saying, "The Sleep Learning Association seems not to be afraid of adverse criticism often received from scientists, representatives of the British Medical Association, and a doctor-journalist," in addition to a cartoon showing a subject kneeling by his bedside, reciting the following:

> *"Matthew, Mark, Luke, and John,*
> *Bless the tape that I lie on,*
> *Let me know, ere daylight comes,*
> *How to do proportion sums."*

The doctor-journalist referred to was the Family Doctor of the *Guardian* newspaper, who had previously written:

"I will believe it when someone shows me scientific evidence that it works." When I wrote back to the *Guardian* about the doctor's remark, the doctor replied: "I would remind Mr. Stocker that a skeptic, as he described me, is one who questions an apparent truth, not one who necessarily disbelieves."

A leading education journal, *New Education,* set about a thorough investigation of the subject. They commissioned a Russian journalist, Villen Lustiberg, to inquire into sleep learning to see "what promise the technique holds for the future." The journalist confirmed all our findings, and described much of the work of Svyadoshch, Bliznitchenko, and other leading scientists described admirably in this book. In the journalist's report, the way to the future was clearly shown.

We were invited to give a lecture on "Hypnopaedia" by Professor H. J. Eysenck, Ph.D., at the Institute of Psychiatry, London University. The address was given by Fredrick Rubin, Research Officer of the Association. Professor Eysenck wrote: "There is evidence that learning is possible during light phases of sleep. Nothing whatever seems to be learned during heavy sleep."

The sleep learning way of learning languages was demonstrated very effectively on the *David Frost Show* on British television before millions of viewers. Mr. Frost personally selected the subject, a young woman known to him who could not speak German. He introduced her to the studio audience, explaining that she would be learning German while asleep every night, and that she would return one week later to be examined by himself. When the young lady, Clo Hack, reappeared the following week she was able to answer questions without hesitation, and even laughed and joked with confidence, speaking only in German. Mr. Frost gave her a score of nine out of a possible ten on some of her answers, and ten out of a possible ten for the remainder. He was greatly surprised and agreed that she spoke fluently and with a good accent.

On another similar occasion, Peter Williams, producer of the *Day by Day* program on southern British television, announced that he intended to learn Spanish by the sleep learning method and show his viewers the various stages of his progress. On the first appearance, we saw Mr. Williams getting into bed in his pajamas, placing a pillow speaker under his pillow, adjusting a time switch and a tape recorder at the side of his bed, nestling down to sleep, and finally, dramatically, turning off the light. After two weeks he was examined by a Spanish linguist from Southampton University. Results again were very impressive. Mr. Williams spoke in Spanish and had memorized almost all of what he had learned with a very good accent.

Another public demonstration of sleep learning was less successful. Bernard Braden, actor/broadcaster, described on his show some of the excellent results obtained from the use of our therapy tapes. He and his wife chose to use a tape called "Stop Smoking!" and arranged to report back to viewers periodically on their progress. The results were negative. They both continued to smoke but admitted that they are very busy people, heavy smokers, and unable to settle down to a regular nightly procedure.

One of our members offered part of her country residence for further experimentation with language teaching. The Centre was opened in Cheltenham, Gloucestershire, where we held residential courses in German, French, Spanish, and Italian.

A year later we opened another Centre in the New Forest, Hampshire, teaching various professional topics for the General Certificate of Education examinations. Many children stayed at the Centre for two to six weeks during their summer holidays, receiving instruction during the day and in the dormitories at night. With this programmed learning, we were able to offer pony rides, swimming, rambling, nature studying, organized games, and picnics, all in the delightful setting of the New Forest.

Almost all the students passed their examinations and praised the courses highly, some doing so on television. The "method" was described at the time as a "breakthrough in education" and the good results were broadcast on television news shows.

Unfortunately, without financial backing we were unable to sustain these early efforts, and the Centres closed. Meanwhile, Russian scientists in the field of sleep learning received grants directly from the Soviet government, and other grants from various education establishments.

Our technicians designed the ideal sleep learning tape recorder, which had a built-in, three-on-off time switch and facilities for silent automatic rewind and replay. Ferguson/HMV were generally interested in our model but considered that there would be insufficient demand to warrant production. A representative of Philips Industries called at one time to discuss the future prospects of sleep learning. Nothing further developed.

Linguaphone discussed the subject of sleep learning at our London Centre and were invited to inspect our dormitories. They were very interested in the amount of popular attention received to date, and did in fact make their own course in French with their own linguists, finally deciding that the project was "not commercially viable."

One or two private boarding schools were also interested and considered our proposal to set up equipment in their dormitories as an experiment. Unfortunately, at the last moment, some parents strongly opposed such "brainwashing" methods and the Governors were forced to step in and cancel all plans.

There is a great future for sleep learning. Governments should come to realize this, as the Russian government did. There is an enormous creative potential within the individual that must be fully exploited. This can only bring greater power to the nation.

We have, so far, only scratched the surface of a vast and most profound subject.

In Great Britain, the education system is in a shambles. And so it is the right time now for governments to organize an official body, say a think tank of the finest brains we can find, to determine *what* we should learn—a very big subject in itself—and *how* we should learn it in the quickest and most effective manner—also a very big subject.

If we set about this now in the '90s, perhaps we shall be ready for the year 2000.

Until the authorities establish such a creative system, it can only be left to each one of us to set about our *own* self-development program, look after our *own* interests and the interests of those near and dear to us, decide what we want to learn, and get down to learning it. In that way we can all best develop our own unique gifts, talents, and abilities—our creative potential.

This book on sleep learning will set you on the right path.

Geoffrey Stocker
London, England

A Note to the Reader

The fascinating technique of sleep learning demands an in-depth understanding of how and why the method works before you, the prospective sleep learner, try it. Without this thorough knowledge, you risk your understanding of the incredible journey on which you are about to embark.

The final chapters of this book contain specific instructions for learning while you sleep. These are the basic mechanical aspects of the process. However, the reader who truly desires to succeed at sleep learning will require far more than the simple mechanics. You must prepare yourself for the experience. Psychological preparation will contribute immeasurably to your success.

The earlier chapters explain how it is possible to learn while asleep, and how that information is processed into memory. The middle chapters describe the variety of ways in which sleep learning has been put to use, including learning foreign languages, shedding unwanted habits or anti-social behavior, and as therapy for mental afflictions.

Because this knowledge will help you to prepare yourself properly, I urge you to read the entire book before you begin sleep learning.

Sleep learning may prove to be the most cost-effective

method for learning. The equipment you'll need is readily available everywhere, and will cost well under $100. You may have some of the required items in your home now.

My research into sleep learning has lasted more than fifteen years and still continues. When you have finished this book and begun practicing sleep learning to acquire knowledge, to overcome bad habits, or for general self-improvement, I would welcome hearing about your experiences. All sleep learners are invited to write to me at the publisher's address listed on the copyright page at the front of this book.

Mr. Geoffrey Stocker of the Sleep Learning Association defined what has since become known as the first law of sleep learning. It is something you should keep in mind when you begin sleep learning:

MOTIVATION + RELAXATION +
CONFIDENT EXPECTATION =
SUCCESSFUL SLEEP LEARNING

James P. Duffy

1

Unlocking Your Mind

Facts and Fictions

For over half a century, scientists of various disciplines have been studying sleep learning in its many forms. Except for a handful of entrepreneurs and some imaginative pioneers who, through trial and error, discovered how to use this remarkable educational tool on their own, sleep learning in the United States has been almost totally confined to the laboratory, the exclusive preserve of scientists and researchers. They have experimented with it from every conceivable angle for every conceivable purpose.

I began research for this book in 1974 and rewrote several sections many times over as new information updated or invalidated existing theories. I interviewed dozens of scientists—psychologists, psychiatrists, physiologists, neurophysiologists, etc. I analyzed hundreds of scholarly papers, reports, articles, and research projects. I engaged in probing discussions with people who have used sleep learning on their own, those who were successful and those not so successful. In the process I unearthed a tangle of information, misinformation, and myths that were repeated so frequently by so many sources they took on the guise of scientific truth.

While analyzing the work of these researchers, it became clear their conclusions fell into one of three categories: (a) sleep learning worked; (b) sleep learning might work; and (c) sleep learning didn't work.

An absence of valid scientific methods appears to characterize the work of those who concluded that sleep learning doesn't work. In fact, many who came to this conclusion seem to have set up their experiments in a manner calculated to arrive at that result from the beginning. One commentator, Richard Deming, concluded in his book *SLEEP: Our Unknown Life* that those scientists who attacked sleep learning did so because they thought it would not work. This was based on personal opinion, though, that was not supported by any sound scientific proof.

Even when these scientists actually conducted controlled experiments, many failed to follow basic guidelines for successful sleep learning programs. They chose subjects who were not motivated to learn, or used inane material such as meaningless nonsense syllables. Sometimes they even disrupted their subjects' sleep patterns. All these tactics seemed designed to deter their subjects from learning anything while they slept. But when proven guidelines were followed, success was unmistakable.

The reluctance of some researchers to take a stronger position in support of sleep learning is understandable, even where the results of their own experiments had been positive. Most men and women of science are trained to think in objective terms. They work in a world of absolutes, a world where every loose end must be closely examined, tested, and tied up. It is not always their function to apply their findings in a practical way. To those of us outside the laboratory environment, it often seems that some researchers would prefer to experiment and test *ad infinitum*.

The need for absolute scientific understanding, added to this reluctance to take a public stand on a potentially controversial issue, can create some amusing situations.

Suppose Dr. Waldo Moss, a fictitious sleep researcher, has just conducted a sleep learning program aimed at teaching several student volunteers the Hindustani translation of a series of English words. The program was a success in that most students learned the translations. Dr. Moss now prepares to write an article for a scientific journal. Through a dozen pages he conscientiously reports every phase and step of his experiment, including the name of the manufacturer of the recording device used and the decibel level at which the lesson was played. At the end of the article, Dr. Moss must present his conclusions. What is the significance of the results he achieved?

Dr. Moss elects to approach this part of his article in a question and answer style. One question he asks is, "Can learning take place during sleep?" Here the cautious scientist emerges. To this question, Dr. Moss replies, "Maybe." He then uses three paragraphs to justify the reply despite the incontrovertible success of the experiment he's writing about.

But even while some researchers have been this overcautious, others have achieved results that ranged from interesting to amazing. As we'll see later, many scientists have proven the validity of sleep learning, and aren't afraid to say so.

I have researched and written other books on other subjects during the past fifteen years, but I kept returning to sleep learning. I was fascinated by a subject with the potential to add an exciting new dimension to how people acquire knowledge. That an individual here or there could successfully practice sleep learning really didn't interest me; I wanted to know if it could work for anyone. The answer to this question, as you will discover once you have completed this book and begun your own sleep learning, is a resounding YES! Thousands of people around the world are successful sleep learners. They use it to learn other languages, stop bad habits such as overeating and nail biting, as a study aid for school lessons, and dozens of other reasons. Hopefully, this book will help millions more become successful sleep learners.

During these years of research, I developed several prerequisites vital to successful sleep learning. They are:

1. The sleep learner must be motivated to learn;
2. the lesson must contain information the person wants to learn;
3. it must be presented at the right times during sleep; and
4. sleep learners must believe in their own potential to learn during sleep.

Several ground rules and guidelines also apply to successful sleep learning. These will be discussed in depth as we progress.

The entire concept of learning while you sleep contradicts many of our assumptions about sleep. Most people are under the misconception that sleep is a period of calm requiring minimal use of their mental functions. Nothing is further from the truth. During sleep, our minds are in a high degree of activity. A small portion of that activity is reflected in dreams and nightmares. The average healthy human has mental capabilities during sleep of which most of us are unaware.

As we'll see in a later chapter, measuring devices reveal that an astonishing amount of mental activity takes place during sleep even while physical functions slow down almost to a stop. In October 1984, Dr. Christian Guilleminault and a group of researchers at Stanford University discovered that the hearts of some healthy young adults actually stopped beating for short periods while they slept.

Scientific research conducted in the United States during the past thirty years and work done at European facilities such as the British Research Centre for the Development of Hypnopaedic Learning has produced enough information to enable us to construct an effective program for individuals who want to learn during sleep. While research continues, the general public can now make use of this accumulated knowledge and begin sleep learning.

The History of Sleep Learning

It should come as no surprise that science fiction writers were among the first to make use of modern sleep learning. In its June 1911 issue, *Modern Electronics,* the world's first radio magazine, boasting a circulation approaching 100,000, carried an installment of a science fiction story by Hugo Gernsback, titled "Ralph 124C 41+." The installment dealt with a wondrous device called the hypnobioscope, an instrument that enabled people to learn while they slept. Here the author describes its use:

> "Before he fell asleep he attached to his head a double leather headband with metal temple plates . . .
> "He then called his faithful butler, and told him 'put on Homer's Odyssey for the night.'
> "All books are read while one sleeps. Most of the studying is done while one sleeps. Some people have mastered ten languages, which they learned during their sleep-life."

Gernsback described the instruments used for learning while asleep in this way:

> ". . . at each end of the (head)band was attached a round metal disc which pressed closely on the temples. From each metal disc an insulated wire led to a small square box, the menograph, or mindwriter. When the start button for the menograph was depressed, immediately a wave line, traced in ink, appeared on a narrow white fabric band."

The menograph described by the author was a primitive description of the electroencephalograph (EEG) used today for sleep-related research. The EEG didn't come into existence until seventeen years later, when it was introduced by a German physiologist, Hans Berger.

Twelve years after the appearance of "Ralph 124C 41+," another magazine, *Radio News,* suggested that what had been perceived as fantasy might in fact be true. The magazine referred to the earlier Gernsback story and related an incident in which the sleep learning theory had actually been tested. According to the article, United States Navy Chief J. N. Phinney claimed to have tried sleep learning on several student sailors at a Pensacola, Florida, training center. He got the idea from an article in the December 1921 issue of *Science and Invention* that mentioned the possibility of learning while asleep.

Phinney said he used sleep learning in December 1922 to see if it would help his students learn the Morse code faster. The Navy instructor claimed remarkable success in this first recorded sleep learning experiment. He reported that the performance of fifteen of the seventeen volunteer sleep learners improved after the nocturnal lessons.

Sleep learning gained a wider audience and a new name in the early 1930s with the publication of Aldous Huxley's *Brave New World*. In his futuristic book, Huxley's imaginary world government used sleep learning, or hypnopaedia, as he called it, for "normal education" and to prepare children for the lifestyle they would live within their pre-selected class of society.

For a description of how Huxley envisioned a world state might use sleep learning, we join the Director of Hatcheries and Conditioning as he tours the Central London Hatchery and Conditioning Center with a newly arrived group of students.

"Fifty yards of tiptoeing brought them to a door which the director cautiously opened. They stepped over the threshold into the twilight of a shuttered dormitory. Eighty cots stood in a row against the wall. There was a sound of light regular breathing and a continuous murmur, as of very faint voices remotely whispering.

"A nurse rose as they entered and came to attention before the Director.

" 'What's the lesson this afternoon?' he asked. 'We had Elementary Sex for the first forty minutes,' she answered. 'But now it's switched over to Elementary Class Consciousness.'

"The Director walked slowly down the long line of cots. Rosy and relaxed with sleep, eighty little boys and girls lay softly breathing. There was a whisper under every pillow. The D.H.C. halted and, bending over one of the little beds, listened attentively."

What the Director of Hatcheries and Conditioning listened to was a portion of the Elementary Class Consciousness lesson. It was this lesson that first attached a connotation of "brainwashing" to sleep learning. How this happened is easily understood by the content of the lesson.

"Alpha children wear gray. They work much harder than we do, because they're so frightfully clever. I'm really awfully glad I'm a Beta, because I don't work so hard. And then we are much better than the Gammas and Deltas.

"Gammas are stupid. They all wear green, and Delta children wear Khaki. Oh no, I don't want to play with the Delta children. And Epsilons are still worse. They're too stupid to be able to read and write. Besides they wear black, which is a beastly color. I'm so glad I'm a Beta."

According to the Director, the sleeping children would hear that lesson between forty and fifty times before they were awakened. Then they could progress to a more advanced lesson. He called sleep learning the "greatest moralizing and socializing force of all time."

A man with a wide range of interests and knowledge, Huxley's interest in sleep learning (or hypnopaedia) never wavered. Over a quarter of a century after the publication of *Brave New World*, he wrote on the subject again. He devoted an entire chapter of his 1958 book, *Brave New World Revisited*, to sleep learning.

This time, Huxley was concerned about the use of sleep learning at a penal institution in California. He was referring to reports that sleep learning was being tested as a means to alter the behavioral patterns of prison inmates. According to these reports, several inmates had volunteered for a program consisting of nightly prerecorded lessons intended to instill in them a desire to turn their backs on crime and lead virtuous lives.

Huxley's concern wasn't with the intent of the messages. "No, it is not the message conveyed by the inspirational whisper that one objects to, it is the principle of sleep teaching by governmental agencies. Is hypnopaedia the sort of instrument that officials ought to be allowed to use at their discretion?" The man who first introduced the term *hypnopaedia* to the general public had reason to be concerned. The use of sleep learning for moralistic purposes sounded too much like an early stage of the "Suggestions from the State," as the Director of Hatcheries and Conditioning called the Elementary Class Consciousness lessons.

Despite reservations about the possible misuse of sleep learning, Aldous Huxley believed the technique could have beneficial applications aside from simply learning. In a letter to his friend, Dr. Humphrey Osmund, Huxley expressed a strong feeling that suggestions made during sleep might be a successful therapy in the treatment of mentally ill patients. In a later chapter, we'll see how much foresight Huxley showed in this direction.

A few years later, Huxley explained how he believed sleep learning worked and how it might aid those suffering from illness.

He believed that verbal suggestions made to a sleeping person enter the brain through the cortex and find their way to the nervous system. He firmly advocated that the bodily functions of a sleeper could be altered if these suggestions made during sleep were repeated often enough and they were conceived properly.

Four and a half years later, Huxley again proposed the use of sleep learning to help in the cure of mental illness. He urged that a process of chemical hibernation of cancer patients be accompanied by suggestions during sleep. His interest in sleep learning for therapeutic applications is quite natural, since Huxley was not only a novelist, but a medical doctor as well.

Although we must credit fiction writers with awakening interest in sleep learning, the concept is actually much older than we might suspect. Several ancient civilizations constructed temples in which followers would periodically come to sleep. Researchers have expressed the belief that the priests of these temples would silently move among the sleeping faithful and whispers religious instructions in their ears.

A leading sleep learning researcher, Professor of Psychiatry A.M. Svyadoshch of the Karaganda State Medical Institute in the U.S.S.R., reports the early use of sleep learning in three countries. According to Svyadoshch, Vetterstrand in Germany in 1893, N. V. Viazemskii in Russia in 1903, and France's Burdon in 1904 all used some form of suggestion during sleep on their patients. Science fiction stories using sleep learning methods, including several by Russian authors, were instrumental in interesting Svyadoshch himself in the subject.

In the post World War II period, extraordinary reports based mostly on unsubstantiated claims of sleep learning success appeared. This sensationalism was in part responsible for the cautious approach to publicity taken by many researchers who worked with sleep learning during the following decades. Along with these exaggerated reports, primitive sleep learning equipment made its appearance in the marketplace.

The year 1947 saw the birth of what grew in eleven years to become a ten-million-dollar industry. By 1958, the sleep learning equipment business was in full swing and many of the claims made by its salesmen grew increasingly outlandish.

Early in 1958, the industry drew the attention of the *Wall Street Journal*, resulting in a front page article on the sleep learning industry. The article, written by a *Journal* staff reporter, repeated some of the claims made by those who were in the business of selling equipment. Most notable of these was that "well over 100,000 people in the United States were successfully using sleep learning." Reference was also made to a two-year investigation of the industry by the Federal Trade Commission. A recent search of the files of the Commission was unable to uncover any information concerning such an investigation.

Another claim was that several U.S. corporations were using sleep learning to train salesmen. The list of companies included the Chrysler Corporation. In an effort to substantiate this, I questioned Mario S. Gorbin, at the time manager of Dealer Relations and Marketing Training for Chrysler. Mr. Gorbin, who had been associated with Chrysler's dealer sales training program since 1953, told me he had no knowledge of sleep learning ever being used. He did say the company once looked into some of the claims made by its advocates, but that was as far as they had gone.

For those concerned with establishing and maintaining the validity of sleep learning, these were the Dark Ages. The tidbits of information that were coming from successful experiments were too often blown out of proportion and became fair game for skeptics who refused to believe sleep learning could work.

This seamy phase of its history should not discourage anyone from using sleep learning. Over the past twenty-five years, tremendous advances have been made in the field. The full potential of sleep learning has not yet been fully realized, nor have all the areas in which sleep learning can make a substantial contribution been identified. Yet we are definitely ready to make practical use of the technique as a tool to improve and enrich our lives.

While sleep learning equipment manufacturers and marketing companies in the United States were premature, Europeans took a different approach to sleep learning. Undaunted by the sensationalists, European scientists pursued their sleep learning experiments. During this period, a group of professionals representing several scientific disciplines founded a non-profit sleep learning research association. Headquartered in London, the group was formed "to encourage the advancement of sleep learning in this country . . . to help individuals to use the method for benefit; to provide opportunities for the exchange of information; and to stimulate cooperation between members." Since then the Sleep Learning Association has served as a clearinghouse for research. It published, or arranged for the publication of, several technical volumes dealing with sleep learning research methods.

European and American researchers succeeded in accomplishing quite a bit with sleep learning, which we will learn in later chapters. After the initial rush of the 1950s subsided, sleep learning researchers have quietly gone about their work. They've built a substantial base of knowledge on which we can extend the practical use of sleep learning.

Defining Sleep Learning

The obvious question asked about sleep learning is, "How does it work?" To help us understand how it works, we need a precise definition of exactly what sleep learning is. This requires a clarification of terms. The method of learning during sleep is called either sleep learning or hypnopaedia, depending on the speaker or writer. The terms are interchangeable. The use of hypnopaedia as a scientific or technical name for sleep learning is a direct reflection of Aldous Huxley's influence on the subject.

The techniques of sleep learning actually apply to acquiring knowledge in two distinct states: total sleep, and deep relaxation. The latter is that state of semiconsciousness just before falling asleep. However, for simplification, we will call learning in both states sleep learning. Only when we are discussing deep relaxation exclusively will that term be used.

As a subject for scientific research, sleep learning reaches into areas in which we have limited knowledge and which create controversy among researchers. While some believe it has universal applications and can be used by the general population, others maintain it needs further research and refinement before people are encouraged to learn while they sleep.

Dr. Ernst Schmidhofer, who has used sleep learning techniques extensively since World War II, thinks the typical researcher's opinion on sleep learning is based less on the results of scientific experiments and more on personal preconceived bias that influences the methods used in conducting experiments. During my research I came to agree with him. I repeatedly reviewed sleep learning projects whose methods appeared aimed at disproving the validity of sleep learning instead of the other way around. Scientific research should be of a positive nature, seeking to prove the existence of unrealized human potentials, not seeking to disprove what has already been established.

When people participate in sleep learning sessions, they are usually asleep in their beds while a tape recorder or other similar instrument is playing a selected lesson. For some, this suggests an image of brainwashing much like that described in Aldous Huxley's book. But real brainwashing techniques have nothing to do with sleep learning. Brainwashing is trying to force-feed information that might otherwise be rejected. To work, brainwashing needs a confused, irrational victim, and the best way to make him that way is to deprive him of sleep. While the sleep learner is nicely tucked away in bed engaged in learning something she desires to learn, the brainwashing victim is denied sleep. The brainwashers may force their victim to stand on his feet or walk around in his brightly illuminated cell for endless days. By doing this, they hope to confuse him enough to eradicate his previously learned views and patterns of behavior, which can be replaced with views and patterns of their own creation.

Learning while asleep requires certain psychological conditioning that only the sleep learner can create. No one can force you to learn anything while asleep. The successful sleep learner must have a genuine desire to learn the material.

Another common misconception about sleep learning is that it is akin to suggestions made to a subject under hypnosis. Unfortunately, the term *hypnopaedia* lends itself to association with hypnosis. Such a relationship might exist if the hypnotic, trance-like state was related to sleep, but it isn't. One researcher who examined the results of numerous experiments measuring the brain activity of sleeping and hypnotized individuals found no conclusive relationship in the brain activity patterns of the two groups. In fact, he concluded the EEG patterns of hypnotized people more closely resembled those of a person who was wide awake instead of one who was asleep.

For a complete professional description of sleep learning, we turn to leading Soviet sleep learning researcher, Professor Leonid A. Bliznitchenko, Director of the Department of Experimental Phonetics at the Potebni Institute of Linguistics:

> "Sleep learning is a process that takes place during natural sleep. It consists of introducing into the human mind information which is processed and memorized while the student is asleep. The sleep learning lesson begins while the student is in deep relaxation and continues after the onset of sleep."

Sleep learning uses the functions of learning, memory, and sleep. All three continue to present scientists with unanswered questions. To understand how sleep learning works, we must examine what we know about them and how they apply to sleep learning. To do this, we need to review what we know about the human subconscious. Understanding the subconscious and the powers it makes available to us will help us understand sleep learning, because sleep learning is based on teaching our subconscious mind instead of our conscious mind.

There is also much we need to know about sleep itself. We need to understand how it is possible to hear things while we sleep, and the role of dreams in the processing or memorizing of information. We should know why learning and memory are not only related to sleep and dreams, but might not exist without them. As you learn more about these subjects and how they relate to sleep learning, your capacity to learn successfully in your sleep will be greatly improved.

After you have acquired a basic knowledge of the four components of sleep learning—sleep, the subconscious, learning, and memory—we will bring them together just as sleep learning does to form a viable learning program.

Only by understanding the powers of the subconscious and the capabilities of our minds while we sleep can we recognize that sleep learning is not what some have called a "revolutionary new method of learning," but simply a way of using abilities that are inherent in each of us.

Francis Bacon wrote that "knowledge itself is power." When it comes to sleep learning, knowledge of the human functions and the processes by which we are able to learn while asleep are even more important than power. Knowledge can mean the difference between successful sleep learning and failure. The following chapters provide the knowledge required for successful sleep learning.

2

The Power of Your Subconscious

Your Subconscious at Work

When we apply the term subconscious to discussions on sleep learning, we actually refer to two of the three portions of the mind identified by Sigmund Freud. According to Freud, the human mind resembles a great iceberg in that only the tip, a minute part of the bulk is visible. He divided the mind into three parts:

1. the conscious, that small portion of the iceberg that's always above the waterline;
2. the pre-conscious, the part that is sometimes above and sometimes below the waterline, depending on the motion of the sea in which the iceberg floats; and
3. the unconscious, that largest of all three parts that remains hidden beneath the water.

Freud's definition of the function of the pre-conscious is that it is the portion of the mind which stores information not necessarily in a person's conscious thought at any given moment, but which can be readily retrieved. For example, suppose someone asked you what clothing you wore last Sunday. Unless you were thinking of those clothes at that precise time, you would need a moment to reflect and think back to remember what you wore. In Freud's view, the memory of that clothing was not in the conscious part of your mind, but in the pre-conscious portion. He saw the unconscious as the largest and most influential of the three. Freud believed the unconscious is the center of influence that determines behaviors such as drives, conflicts, and experiences. As this chapter unfolds, we will see that modern scientific consensus not only agrees with Freud but attributes even greater influence to this portion of the mind.

To simplify our review of sleep learning, we'll combine Freud's pre-conscious and unconscious parts into one all-encompassing section which we will call the subconscious.

In his book *Invention, Discovery, and Creativity*, Professor A. D. Moore called the subconscious "the central mystery of the creative process." While Freud thought of the subconscious as wild and uncontrollable, Morton Prince viewed it "as a great mental mechanism which takes part in an orderly, logical way in all the processes of daily life. . . ." Prince believed this mechanism functions in part as a purveyor of options from which we select the one best suited to a given situation. In other words, the credit for solving problems belongs not to the conscious mind, but the subconscious.

Any serious discussion of sleep learning requires an understanding of the major role that the subconscious plays in both behavior and perception. To gain this understanding we must examine how the subconscious operates. A more detailed understanding of the "surfacing" of the subconscious than that offered by Freud's analogy of the iceberg.

To gain a clear picture of how the subconscious and conscious interact, imagine the subconscious at the end of a long roadway leading into the very center of our being. We can see the conscious mind controlling, or at least occupying, the beginning of the road, serving as a series of roadblocks that partially hinder the flow of information either to or from the subconscious. Under certain circumstances, the roadblock is removed, allowing a free flow of thoughts and ideas. This condition is most prevalent when we're asleep, anesthetized, or during various periods of the day when we're conscious but not directly focused. This last is a state of consciousness we might describe by saying, "My mind was wandering," or "His thoughts are a million miles away."

The transition from a conscious to a subconscious state can be an exciting adventure. Locked away in the subconscious are the accumulated experiences of a lifetime. Our subconscious is a storehouse of memories, ideas, thoughts, sights, and sounds.

Although we are not always aware of it, we all make use of the extraordinary creative abilities of our subconscious. Some unusually perceptive people understand this, and find they are most creative when they can slip into a reverie that reduces the conscious mind's roadblock function. A decline in conscious thought produces a corresponding increase in the subconscious activity of our thought processes.

Most of us have at one time or another slipped into a reverie. This is most common when we are riding in a car, train, bus, or airplane. For a few minutes you sit quietly, staring out the window, looking at the passing scene. Before long, the scenes begin to blur into a stream of unidentifiable objects and colors. Boredom begins to set in as your thoughts become occupied elsewhere. Your mind begins reviewing problems related to your job or home. Soon you are completely oblivious to the scenery speeding past your window. Then someone speaks your name. Suddenly you snap out of your preoccupation and return to conscious thought, momentarily stunned by the radical change. This abrupt intrusion on your period of private thoughts could make you feel as if you've just been rudely aroused from a sound sleep.

The person who has brought you back to conscious thought probably felt you were "deep in thought" or perhaps "had a faraway look" in your eyes. What actually occurred was that your conscious mind entered a state of relaxation or reduced vigilance and your subconscious took control of your thought process. The roadblocks established by the conscious mind were pushed aside.

One writer likened this change from conscious to subconscious thought to changing gears in an automobile with a standard transmission. He said it was slipping the clutch. You disengage the motor and get into a mood of no thought. You are relaxed or detached. You turn off your conscious mind and just coast, allowing the subconscious to do the work.

There are several ways to experience this change. Some people say they simply "lie down and relax, letting my mind wander," while others occupy their conscious mind with simple tasks that permit their subconscious to "surface." Others remove themselves physically from their environment by taking a walk with no real destination planned. Many runners report a surge of creative or problem-solving thoughts while they run.

Fashion designer Bonnie Cashin developed a unique way of calling on her subconscious to help overcome difficult problems with her work. Ms. Cashin "prowls" around sections of New York City with no particular goal, or she'll visit the United Nations, sit in the visitor's gallery, and listen to the speakers, even though she doesn't understand their languages.

During sleep, the conscious mind is diminished to its lowest natural level, while the subconscious mind continues to function normally, taking in any sounds that are going on around us. At this time, the subconscious has the greatest control over thought because there is little or no interference from the conscious mind. In these terms we can better understand the reasoning behind the expression, "I want to sleep on it." What we're really saying is that we want to give our subconscious an opportunity to evaluate the situation and offer available options before we select a course of action.

Dr. Herman Baruch, a psychologist, said his famous brother, financial wizard and Presidential advisor Bernard Baruch, had an exceptionally well-developed subconscious. "He goes to sleep at night thinking about a problem and wakes up with the right answer."

These examples do not necessarily mean that the subconscious is active only during periods of drowsiness, boredom, or sleep. Actually, it never stops working. During these states, we are better able to draw on the subconscious' ability to clarify our thoughts, and on its creative powers. This is because they create a condition in which our conscious mind is also in relaxation and isn't performing its roadblock function.

There is a simple explanation why the subconscious acts as a storehouse of our entire life's experiences. It absorbs everything that it witnesses, without the discrimination exercised by the conscious mind. In many ways it is similar to a sponge that literally "soaks up" everything to which the senses are subjected.

The mind has the power to discriminate among the many things that attempt to enter our conscious thought, and turn away those that do not interest us. Our subconscious enjoys no such advantage. It cannot be commanded to ignore. It retains everything. Because it absorbs information continuously and we are unable to regulate its intake, the subconscious is susceptible to external suggestion. Incorrect suggestions can lead to erroneous conclusions when making decisions.

The dividing line between the conscious mind, which we theoretically control through our ability to discriminate, and the subconscious is called the "threshold of awareness." The ability of another person or other outside force to cross that threshold with a suggestion was first identified in 1917 by an Austrian neurologist named Poetzl. In the intervening years, this power, called "suggestion below the threshold," has had tremendous impact on our lives and society.

Making a suggestion that's intended to bypass the natural restraint of the conscious mind is known by three names: subconscious perception, strobonic injection, and subliminal perception. These methods have been widely used to convey a message we might otherwise choose to ignore. The most common application of these types of suggestions is in commercial advertising.

Although many of us are unaware, we see this type of advertising constantly. We see it in the movie star, famous athlete, or other personality who tries to sell us a car, a can of foot deodorant, or a soft drink. Consciously we are aware such testimonials are bought and paid for by advertising agencies. The aim of this advertising is to implant in our subconscious a suggestion of association. When we are shopping and see that brand of foot deodorant or soft drink on a shelf, the advertiser hopes we'll associate that brand with the personality. If we like the personality, we like the brand. Seeing the brand stimulates the good feelings we might have for the personality. The advertising goal is to get us to transfer those good feelings to the deodorant, even if we have never used it.

If you question the validity of this approach to advertising, ask yourself three questions: Why do advertisers pay huge fees to celebrities to give testimonials for their products? When was the last time you saw a product testimonial by a personality who was widely disliked, or was known to have unpopular political or social views? How many of these testimonials refer only to superficial aspects of the product and never tell us anything about its true worth?

The tennis star whose name and testimonial is attached to a brand of tennis clothes rarely tells us how good the material is or how strong the stitching is. He or she may not even know. The appeal is purely superficial. It aims to establish a subconscious association between a champion tennis player and the clothing, as if clothes were a major factor in winning a match.

A more insidious method used to gain access to our subconscious, one more powerful than suggestion by association, is subliminal projection. Here a message of which we may not even be aware enters directly into our subconscious.

In 1956, a projector for delivering such messages was installed in a New Jersey movie theater, in what is conceded to be the first commercial use of subliminal, projection. During a six-week run of the movie *Picnic*, two messages aimed below the threshold of awareness were flashed on the theater's screen for one three-thousandths of a second. The messages read, "Hungry? Eat popcorn," and "Drink Coca-Cola."

The people behind this advertising, Subliminal Projection Co., refused to release information on the effectiveness of their campaign. They did acknowledge an increase in Coca-Cola and popcorn sales during the six weeks. One can only wonder if they concealed a tremendously successful method for selling products for fear of arousing public anger.

The Federal Communications Commission claims similar subliminal projection commercials were tried at several television stations around the country. When this practice became known, the FCC received an avalanche of complaints as well as expressions of grave concern from members of Congress. In an effort to forego the publicity that would accompany FCC or Congressional action, the National Association of Broadcasters banned the use of subliminal projection advertising on television. In the months preceding this ban, several members of the House of Representatives introduced a bill "to make unlawful the use of subliminal advertising on television."

The TV Code of the NAB now prohibits the use of "any technique whereby an attempt is made to convey information to the viewer by transmitting messages below the threshold of normal awareness. . . ." Despite this, the NAB and the FCC became aware of a television commercial used during the 1973 Christmas selling season that contained a subliminal message. It commanded: "Get it!", referring to the product. When this was discovered, the advertising agency responsible for the ad immediately notified all television stations that a new print was being sent. The new print omitted the "Get it!" message aimed at the viewers' subconsciouses.

Everyone is susceptible to this type of suggestion. It is impossible to turn off our subconscious and, as we've seen, there are many who would seek to profit from this.

I am personally aware of a slightly different use of subliminal projection. A movie theater owner showed me a strip of film that was used not to sell a product but to increase a theater audience's reaction to a horror movie. Interspersed throughout the film were individual frames of a particularly gruesome sight unrelated to the story. Pictured in these frames was a human skull with threatening snakes crawling around and through the eye and mouth openings. When the movie was shown, this scene was not visible to the viewer's eyes, for it was aimed below the threshold of awareness. Successful contact with the audience's subconscious would increase the fright aspect of the movie, which would help sell more tickets. This is probably one reason the movie was such a success.

The techniques used by advertisers and promoters are aimed primarily at our subconscious while we are awake and still influenced by the discriminatory powers of our conscious mind.

Access to our subconscious increases when our conscious mind is relaxed. Aldous Huxley described this when he wrote, "In a word, the lower the level of a person's psychological resistance, the greater will be the effectiveness of (these) suggestions."

In relation to sleep learning, we will want to know when that "psychological resistance" is lowest. This occurs when we're in a state of deep relaxation or sleep. Our subconscious is most receptive to suggestions during this period of reduced resistance. This is especially true if we're prepared ourselves to accept the suggestions. As we've seen in previous examples, others are attempting to influence our subconscious for profit. We as individuals can turn similar techniques to our own benefit and self-enrichment. Sleep learning offers the opportunity to do just that. Using sleep learning techniques, we can harness the powers of our subconscious more fully and avail ourselves more effectively of our subconscious memories.

In his book, *Defective Memory, Absentmindedness and Their Treatment*, Doctor Arnold Lorand explained how information enters the subconscious memory. He said most of the information in our subconscious memory enters it through the subconscious mind, bypassing the control of logical understanding. He then went on to say that information enters the subconscious most easily when we are not fully conscious. In this state the subconscious is most receptive because there is no resistance from the conscious mind.

Sigmund Freud said the same thing in a different way.

"The state of sleep makes the formation of dreams possible because it reduces the power of the endopsychic censorship."

We have seen how the subconscious receives outside suggestions and affects our problem-solving and creative abilities. The next step is to determine how long information is stored in the subconscious memory.

A simple description of the difference between our conscious and subconscious memories is that the subconscious memory is almost a mechanical procedure. Our conscious memory operates on judgement, so we usually remember only those things we want to remember. Our conscious judgement is evident in all decisions we make. When someone suggests that we take a certain course of action, we weigh the suggestion in our conscious mind. What we decide depends on the judgement of our conscious mind using the information stored in our conscious memory, which supplies our reasoning power with its knowledge.

Accepting a suggestion will usually be based on the positive—or lack of negative—input from the conscious memory. It might also depend on a lack of stored knowledge.

The knowledge of right and wrong, legal and illegal, moral and immoral is stored in our conscious memory. This knowledge, combined with our experiences, is the root of our decisions. Of course they have little to do with character. Our conscious memory can't force us to do what's right. When we make a decision, the contribution of our conscious memory is affected by our character, our desires, and our ambitions.

The Center of Creativity

Besides serving as a warehouse of memories, the subconscious provides a source of inspiration. Earlier we saw how some people are able to make use of their subconscious ability to solve problems or contribute to artistic creations. For example, Bonnie Cashin sits in the United Nations gallery listening to speakers whose language she doesn't understand. These creative individuals discovered methods to tap the latent talent of their subconscious mind.

They are not alone. Many of us have experienced this subconscious creativity, unaware of the process we have gone through.

We are actually speaking of two talents, separate yet related. They are creativity and problem solving. Dr. Erich Neumann described the creative person as one who is dependent on being receptive to his or her subconscious. He puts the creative person in a separate category from the average individual because the average person adapts to the community. Dr. Neumann believes the conventional person gives up some creativity in order to adapt, while the creative person develops away from the community as he relates more to his own subconscious. Perhaps this forms the basis for the generally held perception that the creative writer, artist, or scientist is "different" from the rest of us. "Oddball" is not an uncommon term used to describe a creative person.

Arthur Koestler called the creative powers of the subconscious mind a different level of thinking. He described his view of the creative process as descending from the conscious level to retrieve an idea from the subconscious.

Two psychologists explored the creative experiences of people from various professions. Based on interviews of twenty-three individuals in a wide range of occupations who had been judged to be especially creative, they concluded that intuition, unconscious promptings, and unexplainable insights play a significant role in the arts and sciences.

One professor divides the process into four phases:

1. preparation, done through the conscious mind;
2. incubation, in which the subconscious develops the correct solution or combination of solutions by searching the warehouse of information;
3. illumination, the transference of the solution from the subconscious to the conscious; and
4. verification, when the conscious mind applies its logic and discriminatory powers to analyze the information received and verify the correct problem has been solved.

Another professor of education at Columbia University described the creative process as pushing an unsolved problem out of the conscious mind and allowing the subconscious to work on it.

Mathematicians are usually thought of as individuals with calculating, logical minds who would probably consider a discussion of the creative subconscious as too subjective to concern them. Yet mathematicians often call on the same creative forces associated with artists and poets.

We cannot calculate the contributions of subconscious creativity to the arts and sciences. But, we can safely say that it is likely that more discoveries have been made by people in a relaxed state than by those slaving over a hot Bunsen burner. The work done in the laboratory or at the writing desk generally amounts to the preliminary portion of the preparation phase within the creative process. Before closing this chapter, we'll examine two examples of how relaxation and free association have provided the incubation phase for creative solutions and ideas.

Harold Black wrestled with the problems of the early vacuum tube at Bell Laboratories. Although by 1927 the tube had found several uses, it was not a good amplifier because it distorted the signals transmitted through it. For several years, Black made no real progress with this problem, until one morning crossing the Hudson River on the Lackawanna Ferry. As Black gazed out at the morning mist covering the river, the solution suddenly flashed into his mind: negative feedback. By a stroke of fate, the morning newspaper he was reading had an entire page erroneously left blank. The page provided ample space on which to draw the circuit that led to the solution of the distortion problem.

The eminent early twentieth-century poet and scholar Alfred E. Housman provides an amusing and different approach to using subconscious creativity.

> "Having drunk a pint of beer at luncheon—beer is a sedative to the brain and my afternoons are the least intellectual portion of my life—I would go for a walk of two or three miles. As I went along thinking of nothing in particular, only looking at things around me and following the progress of the seasons, there would flow into my mind, with sudden and unaccountable emotion, sometimes a line or two of verse, sometimes a whole stanza of verse, accompanied, not preceded, by a vague notion of the poem which they were destined to form part of."

Housman went on to say that an hour or so of a lull would follow. Occasionally this would be followed by another flow of verse. Being unfamiliar with subconscious creativity, the poet attributed the source of this "bubbling up" of ideas as the "pit of the stomach."

We've dealt with the creative center that is the subconscious mind. We've seen that this creativity takes place primarily when an individual is relaxing, distracted, or free associating. Two phenomena on which we haven't touched, but in which the subconscious plays an important role, are sleep dreams and daydreams. The former, because they play an important role in sleep learning, will be treated separately in Chapter IV. Daydreams generally occur during periods of relaxation and are likely connected in some way to the creative process. The internationally known author Isaac Bashevis Singer expressed his opinion of daydreams and creativity in one sentence, "Daydreaming and writing are very, very much connected."

Subconscious Learning

Now that we have some knowledge of the subconscious and its importance, let's see how it can help us. We want to know how sleep learning makes use of this wondrous "inner mind" and its memory.

There are two ways information is communicated to our subconscious. Both employ the two most dominant of the five physical senses. First is through visual messages, both those of which we are aware and the subliminal kind. Second is through verbal messages, again, those we are aware of hearing and those we aren't. Sleep learning is a proven method of communicating verbal messages to our subconscious.

One expert points out that a prerequisite to communicating with the subconscious is diminishing the resistance of the conscious mind. Under normal circumstances, subconscious learning is random. The sleep learner's goal is to harness that randomness and direct selected information into the subconscious.

The self-suggestion techniques used for subconscious learning are most productively applied while the conscious mind is relaxed. The best opportunity to do this is when we are in the drowsy state preceding sleep, and of course, during sleep itself. In both of these states the subconscious mind has "surfaced" and reduced the road-blocks set up by the conscious mind.

Once in pre-sleep, repeat the desired message aloud over and over again. This message could be anything from a mathematical formula to a suggestion for self-improvement aimed at weight reduction or breaking a smoking habit. This repetition, along with the diminished resistance that occurs when the conscious mind is drowsy, will help lower the conscious roadblocks. This method of subconscious learning brings two forces to bear on the conscious mind; the drowsiness of pre-sleep, and the mental monotony produced by repetition. Each of these can reduce conscious resistance independently, but in combination they are especially effective. With relaxation and proper timing, the first five or ten repetitions will remain in the conscious mind and those following will bypass it and go directly to the subconscious.

This procedure is a variation of techniques used for centuries by yogis and mystics for disciplined meditation. A study conducted by Japanese scientists found that the brain waves of a Zen meditator, as he balances between instant alertness and deep relaxation, are identical to those of a person on the threshold of sleep. The meditator who is able to control or alter bodily functions is believed to be accomplishing these feats through a means of communication with his "inner mind."

There is one major difficulty with this method of subconscious learning: the requirement that the subject remain relaxed while repeating the message. Repeating the information aloud interferes with the ability to relax, and vice versa. An effective remedy for this is to record the message on a device that will replay it over and over, automatically. Having done that, all the subconscious learner need do is switch on the device before falling asleep so it continues to broadcast the message while the learner slips into deep relaxation and, finally, sleep itself.

This method will supply the continuous repetitions needed to aid the transformation into diminished conscious resistance and learning. It also avoids the problem of repeating the message aloud while trying to avoid conscious awareness of it. The recorded message makes the entire process easy.

A further benefit of a recorded message is that it will continue broadcasting after the learner has fallen asleep. Without the recording, the message would stop before sleep was actually reached. Because it's during sleep that conscious resistance is least effective, it's important that the message continue to be transmitted to the subconscious while the learner is asleep.

A second approach to subconscious learning is the subliminal visual message. Earlier we saw how some people have attempted to profit by introducing this type of suggestion to the subconscious of others. As we'll now see, this approach can be put to more constructive use.

A New York City psychoanalyst experimented with subliminal projection and found that the subconscious mind is capable of seeing things of which we are consciously unaware. He used a projector that flashes a scene for one one-hundredth of a second, too fast for the human eye to see. Not one person he tested could see the scenes projected, yet the same scenes later appeared in their dreams. What their conscious minds had been unable to see visually, their subconscious minds had been able to perceive and then reproduce later while they slept.

Intrigued, the psychoanalyst tried the same test again. This time he used a different set of scenes someone else selected for him, and tried it on himself. The results were the same. He couldn't see what was projected before him, yet the same scenes became part of his sleeping dreams. Then he drew the scenes he remembered from his dreams. He describes how it feels to reproduce images introduced into his dreams through his subconscious:

"When one makes drawings of the scenes, they seem to come out of the pencil, almost like automatic writing—the pencil draws by itself. Along with the automatic quality there is a compulsive need to put in or omit certain items."

Two key phrases are, "they seem to come out of the pencil" and "a compulsive need." Considering that these feelings were expressed by a man educated to analyze experiences and correctly describe them, there can be little doubt that the drawings were a product of his subconscious.

This experience proves that the subconscious can "see" what we cannot see, and that not only can it insert what it has seen into our dreams, it can also direct us to reproduce the image physically. The results of these experiments confirmed the discovery of Otto Poetzl, inventor of the projector used in these tests. During World War I, the Austrian used his invention to flash scenes before a group of people who reported they did not see them, but later described the same scenes when relating their dreams.

The basic difference in the delivery of visual and audio subliminal messages is the conditions existing when the processes takes place. As we've seen, we can be subconsciously aware of visual images while we are fully awake and in control of our senses, but the subliminal message must appear so quickly that it is just beyond our ability to see it. The audio message can be broadcast within what we consider our normal hearing range, but it is best used when we are asleep, or when we are in drowsy pre-sleep relaxation.

When we are properly motivated, sleep learning helps us take advantage of our reduced conscious resistance while we sleep, without having to reach beyond our normal hearing range. This is exactly what takes place when we learn while we sleep. Even if our conscious mind is asleep when we are, our subconscious can receive and process information. Many people do it every night without even knowing it. Sleep learning lets us manage this natural process by controlling the information we receive while we sleep.

In the next chapter, we will discuss learning and memory, two functions of receiving and processing information. How we process, or memorize, information is important to a thorough understanding of sleep learning.

Before going on, however, we should mention one other type of subconscious learning many people experience regularly. This takes the form of conditioning our subconscious to react in a certain way to an event occurring at a later time. An example of this is a person who is able to awaken at a specific time without the aid of an alarm clock. One way to do this is by force of habit. The person who awakens at the same time each day for a long period will usually awaken at that same time even if he forgets to set the alarm clock. A habit of awakening every day at 6 A.M. can train the subconscious to arouse us at that time. People who can awaken at a pre-arranged time without an alarm clock are said to have an "inner alarm clock." Actually they have made use of an ability we all have, subconscious learning.

3

How We Learn and Remember

The Conditions for Learning

Learning and memory are inseparable. Without memory there can be no learning. The traditional method of evaluating how much someone has learned is to test that person's ability to recall the information they've learned. If nothing is recalled, then nothing has been learned.

Professor Robert Cagne established three conditions that must exist if learning is to take place. They are:

1. motivation;
2. attention; and
3. developmental readiness.

All three are primarily internal conditions, or states of mind. According to Cagne, they are the most important factors in a student's preparation to learn which can be influenced by an instructor.

Since sleep learning is a method of learning, to understand it requires an understanding of how we learn.

Professor Cagne's conditions apply even more to sleep learning than to traditional methods of learning. In many respects, sleep learning students are self instructors, who must exercise a strong influence on their own preparation for the learning experience.

Most educators agree motivation is the most important condition affecting a student's ability to learn. However, there are several types of motivation. Cagne believes the one most relevant to successful learning is "motivation to engage in learning." He call this establishing an intention to learn or a "learning set." This is especially important in sleep learning.

Several factors contribute heavily to create this motivation. They are external conditions that are, for the most part, products of our own lifestyles, needs, and goals. First is social pressure. This is the desire to win the approval of others, such as relatives, friends, or fellow workers. Second is the desire for mastery. This usually relates to skills that are generally considered intellectual in nature. Finally, there is the desire for achievement, which contributes to the self-motivation of those people who, for their own satisfaction, constantly strive for higher levels of skills and knowledge. These are the self-motivators.

Many students participate in the educational process because they are required by law to attend school, or are pressured by their parents to "get a good education." Neither reason produces a reliable motivation to learn. Although it's possible to acquire knowledge without motivation, the highly successful student is generally extremely well motivated.

In the next two chapters, we'll see examples of the amazing powers of judgment that are present during sleep. By establishing the proper learning set through genuine motivation to learn, we can control this judgment capability and allow the sleep learning lesson to be absorbed thoroughly into our subconscious memory. Without adequate motivation, it is doubtful if much of the lesson will be learned.

A properly motivated sleep learner actually experiences a form of subconscious learning even before the first lesson begins. This is accomplished by instructing the subconscious on what it should consider important information. A classic example of highly motivated subconscious learning is the mother of an infant who instructs her subconscious to awaken her if the infant cries, but not when extraneous sounds occur, such as a truck passing her bedroom window. A sleep learning student accomplishes the same thing by being truly motivated to learn the material to be presented in the nocturnal lesson.

The successful student's close attention to the subject is of optimum importance to learning. The student who spends a majority of classroom time looking out the window is sure to learn less than the student who directs full attention to the instructor. Psychologists define attention as "the selectivity of the perceptual processes." Put in simpler terms, we respond unequally to different things we perceive.

For example, we may focus our attention on some objects in a scene while ignoring others. The outstanding characteristics of objects that command our attention are known as "attention getters." Usually, there is something unique about these objects. Contrast and movement are visual attention getters, while volume and pitch are auditory attention getters. We can see examples of their effectiveness everyday. A roadside billboard or a newspaper advertisement will be arranged so that the attention-getting words or objects are most prominently displayed. The word FREE is never buried in the text of an ad and may be the largest attention-getting word in the English language. Some companies will even incur extra expense to animate billboards to attract attention.

A brilliant example of an attention-getting billboard is the famous cigarette smoker over New York's Times Square. Actually nothing on the billboard (which is the face of a person smoking) moves, but every few seconds a giant smoke ring emits from the smoker's mouth.

Television viewers often complain that commercials are louder than the regular programming. Although broadcasters decline to discuss this, the higher volume is a method to gain viewers' attention during commercials.

A humorous story about attention getting tells of a farmer who hit his donkey on the head with a large board. A passing stranger, seeing this, asked if the donkey was refusing to move. "No," answered the farmer, "before I can tell him to move I have to get his attention." Fortunately, paying attention to a sleep learning lesson requires no such drastic action. The environment in which most of us sleep is normally void of distractions. If an attention problem exists for the sleep learner, it will generally occur at the start of the lesson.

For most sleep learners, motivation to learn will eliminate the need for attention-getting devices, because it will help them anticipate the lesson. For those who find self-motivation isn't enough, two methods are helpful in focusing their attention. Whenever possible, sleep learning students should prerecord the lesson personally. The sound of one's own voice is an attention getter in itself. A second is the frequent mention of the sleeper's name. In several sleep learning programs, lists of names were read to sleeping subjects, who reacted more positively to the mention of their own name. We'll deal with this in more detail later.

Professor Cagne describes the final condition, developmental readiness, as the stage a person must reach before specific kinds of learning can take place. For a sleep learner, this stage is determined by what you already know and by how much you have to learn in order to reach your goal.

For example, let's suppose a group of young children are being taught the abstract rules of calculus. They can't possibly be successful unless they have first mastered the concepts and equations of algebra. Such prerequisites are important at any level of learning. Complex skills are learned faster when the simpler skills that relate to them are mastered first.

Developmental readiness applies more to the subject of the lesson than to the method of teaching, and is influenced by the abilities of each individual student. It may not be completely necessary to meet this pre-condition for sleep learning. The number of verified sleep learning cases in which foreign languages were learned by people totally unfamiliar with them is ample evidence of this. Since language learning while asleep is best used for conversational purposes, there's little need to get into the complexities of grammar.

Learning is acquiring knowledge or skill. The amount of knowledge or skill we learn is judged by what we remember. Retaining what we have been taught is the acid test of the learning process. A student takes periodic examinations to test the amount of knowledge he or she has acquired. A quality control inspector in a factory checks the products made by workers to insure they're performing in accordance with the skills acquired through their training. These are forms of testing what has been learned and retained. An individual who is unable to retain anything is also unable to acquire knowledge and skills.

How We Remember

It is no exaggeration to say that memory is everything. Without memory we couldn't "learn." We wouldn't have intelligence or a past. Since memories are an individual's stored record of experiences, they are the individual.

There has always been disagreement among experts about the process of memorization. Several theories exist about the function of remembering, both the original storing of information and the recall of it at a later time. It is possible that someday researchers will identify several depositories for memory. Some of these may prove to be temporary storerooms of information where data is evaluated and processed before being integrated into permanent memory or discarded.

The irony surrounding our lack of knowledge about the processes that permit us to learn and remember was expressed by D. S. Halacy, Jr., in his book, *Man and Memory*: "We can understand anything—except the facility that makes all else understandable."

Two respected brain and memory researchers give us an example of the differences of opinion that plague their field. Dr. Karl Lashley trained a group of rats to find their way through a set of mazes. When they learned this task sufficiently, he surgically removed a different portion of the cortical region of the brain from each rat. When they recovered from surgery, the rats were returned to the maze.

Lashley tested each rat individually to determine its ability to remember how to solve the maze. If a rat was unsuccessful, it could be assumed to have no memory of the previous training, which would indicate the portion of its brain that had been removed contained its memory. To Lashley's surprise, every rat found its way out of the maze. Despite the fact some were maimed from surgery, the rats crawled through the maze just as they had remembered it. The results prompted Lashley to conclude that memory was not stored in the cortex. It had to be stored elsewhere.

Dr. Wilder Penfield found that by lightly touching areas of a human's cortex with a probe, he could stimulate memories believed to have long been "lost." This seemed to indicate that memory storage was located within the cortex. He concluded that the brain was like a magnetic tape that permanently affixed memory to itself, and all that was required to play it back was pushing the proper button on the recorder, or in this case, applying pressure to the right spot on the cortex.

In 1885, the German psychologist Hermann Ebbinghaus published the results of almost twenty years of research and experimentation on memory. Considered by many to be the father of memory research, Ebbinghaus plotted a "memory curve" which effectively demonstrated that the level of retention declines rapidly at first, then levels off to a constant amount.

Ebbinghaus used himself as a subject in one experiment. While in his mid-thirties, he memorized the poem "Don Juan." His goal was to test his theory that in spite of a short-term rapid loss of most of the poem, some portion of it would never be lost from his memory. Twenty-two years later he was unable to consciously recall any lines of the poem, so he decided to learn it over again. He was able to re-learn "Don Juan" at a much faster rate the second time. This faster rate of learning convinced him that at least some parts of the poem remained in his memory, but he had been unable to retrieve them. He attributed his increased re-learning rate to dormant memory.

Ebbinghaus' work resulted in two concepts of learning. One is re-learning. This means once something is learned it is never completely forgotten. Although it may not be recalled easily, it will enhance a later effort to re-learn the same material. The other concept is over-learning. This is based on the premise that repetition is essential for the mastery of the material to be learned. To over-learn, it is necessary to know how many repetitions an individual needs to memorize something. For example, if learning four lines of poetry requires twenty repetitions, most students will reach this point and stop studying, assuming they have successfully learned the poem. Applying the concept of over-learning, dozens of researchers since Ebbinghaus have proven that the student who continues the repetitions beyond this point has better recall than the student who stops at twenty. The more repetition, the better it's learned.

The importance we place on a "good memory" is confirmed by the amount of money spent each year by tens of thousands of people who purchase books and tape recordings aimed at improving memory. Many of the suggestions offered can be used successfully by most readers, while others are of dubious value.

We've all been impressed by individuals with a "photographic memory," or "total recall," as they answer difficult questions with apparent ease. Many famous people have shown tremendous capacity for memory. Arturo Toscanini is said to have been able to conduct symphonies without the help of written scores, having committed them to memory. General George Marshall could discuss minute details of events of World War II years after the war ended. One admirer described Marshall's memory in this way: "He organized and arranged facts in his mind as he did soldiers in the field."

In Swift's *Gulliver's Travels*, the Master of the Mathematical School taught his pupils by writing each lesson on a wafer with special ink. When students swallowed the wafer, the chemicals in the ink made their way to the student's brain, thus imparting knowledge. A wafer with magic ink or a pill that would improve memory after being swallowed has been an age-old fantasy of mankind.

Besides the factors discussed earlier, motivation to learn, whether by traditional methods or through sleep learning, is influenced by our personal feelings about the subject matter. The degree to which we're able to recall information we've heard or read can be directly affected by our bias concerning that information. Our memorization process can discriminate against statements with which we disagree, and in fact, reject such material entirely. This memory selectivity also takes place when we are exposed to verbal, written, or visual material in which we have no interest.

As we saw earlier, this discrimination is a product of the conscious portion of our mind. In most situations, it causes no real problem to avoid memorization of material in which we have no interest. Formal education is an exception. Students taking required courses in which they have little interest don't do as well as they do with courses that stimulate their imaginations and desire for knowledge.

The process of memorizing begins with the desire to learn and remember. If there is no genuine interest to learn, the material is less likely to be memorized and, therefore, will not be learned. We see the evidence of this every day. We constantly hear, see, and experience things that are never committed to our memory. The reason we don't memorize these events is simply that we don't have the desire to do so. Either they hold no meaning or, if they do, we may decide that knowing where the information can be retrieved is sufficient.

The importance of memory to learning was expressed by Dr. Ian Steele Russell of London University College, when he wrote, "The phenomena of memory and learning are inseparable: memory without learning is no more feasible than is learning without memory."

Repeating to Remember

The two components indispensable to learning are the capacity to acquire knowledge or skill and the ability to memorize that knowledge or skill. When we're concerned with acquiring knowledge that can be verbalized, as in sleep learning, the key to memorization is repetition.

Repetition as a means of remembering is used more frequently than we may realize. A common example is the child sent to the grocery store by his mother. Most parents will not trust many purchases to a child's memory, so they will write the items wanted on a piece of paper. If only a few items are to be purchased, a parent may rely on the child remembering them. Usually the mother will repeat the description of the purchase to the child several times then have him or her repeat the list back to her.

Shortly the child is on the way to the grocery store, repeating the list over and over, ''One quart of milk, one loaf of bread, one-half pound of butter. One quart of milk, one loaf of bread, one-half pound of butter . . .'' The repetition helps insure nothing is forgotten.

A reader is struck by something she wishes to remember and reads it over several times until she believes she will be able to repeat it accurately. In both instances, repetition is used to enhance the process of memorizing.

If we could interrupt the reader or the child and inquire why they were repeating the material, they would most likely reply they were trying to ''know it by heart.'' Even today we persist in the use of this term that originated in an age when people believed that functions of the mind originated in the heart.

Although repetition is the most common tool for memorizing something, there are others that can be equally effective. Memorization can be activated by emotional reinforcement. An event that arouses our emotions lodges itself in our memory with a degree of strength similar to that produced by repetition. If we witness a fire, the scene remains in our memory for an extended time. If the fire was especially spectacular, with considerable damage or loss of life, the scene is riveted even more vividly in our memory. The power of emotional reinforcement to produce strong memorization is enhanced by higher levels of emotional stimulation.

Emotional reinforcement has a residual effect of increasing our recall of events that preceded the one arousing our emotions. For example, we might remember what took place the morning preceding the afternoon fire, but can't recall the events of the morning of the day following the fire. Almost everyone has experienced this type of memory reinforcement. Except for those too young to be emotionally affected by the assassination of President John F. Kennedy, most of us can still recall many of the details of our own activities on November 22, 1963. Yet few can recall details of November 21, 1963.

In 1965, the Northeastern states suffered a massive power failure that left millions without power for hours. For several years after, conversations throughout the states involved were sprinkled with ''what were you doing during the blackout'' stories. Memories of activities and events occurring during the power outage survived a long time because they were emotionally reinforced.

For most of us, the recollection of our activities the day Kennedy was assassinated remained ''fixed'' in our memory longer than those of the blackout, due to the higher degree of emotional stimulation. Regardless of one's feelings about Kennedy the politician, the sudden, violent death of the President of the United States was an event with enormous emotional impact. It had a strong influence on our memories every bit as effective as repetition.

However, in the learning process, repetition remains the critical factor. This is why successful sleep learning lessons rely heavily on multiple repetitions of the information or instructional material being broadcast.

Remembering and Forgetting

In recent years, several new theories have been proposed as to why we remember some material while some is forgotten. Most were discarded or disproved through experimentation and practical application. The most widely supported rationale for why we forget something we want to remember is based on interference. This belief is based on the rule, "Interference during learning and after learning reduces the amount of material that can be recalled." Interference is also a major factor in successful sleep learning.

Paradoxically, the primary type of interference that hinders learning is additional learning. An example of this sort of interference is the learner's inability to memorize a long list of words. At some point the list becomes too long to allow the student to memorize all the words. There are too many words, or "too much to learn." When too much material is presented, the later material interferes with learning and memorizing the earlier material.

Interference after learning is also created by additional learning, although the new learning may take place at a later time. Let's take a look at the students who study in the afternoon, right after school. When homework is completed, many students will spend their evenings watching television or listening to records. These activities can be classified as learning that interferes with the processing of information learned earlier, both at school and during home study. The same applies to material learned during the early and late parts of the school day. Each interferes with the other.

Interference of earlier learning on the retention of later learning is known as proactive inhibition. This simple equation was devised to measure the degree of proactive inhibition on individuals:

| Group I | Learn A | Learn B | Recall B |
| Group II | Rest | Learn B | Recall B |

To calculate the effect of proactive inhibition, subtract what Group I recalls of B from what Group II successfully recalls. If both groups have equal recall ability, Group II will do a better job of recalling B because that's all it has learned. There's no prior information to be processed.

The second type of interference is called retroactive inhibition. This applies to the example of the students who watch television after studying. It's the interference of subsequent learning on the retention of material previously learned. By making several minor changes in the equation used for proactive inhibition, we can devise one for retroactive inhibition:

| Group I | Learn A | Rest | Recall A |
| Group II | Learn A | Learn B | Recall A |

The recall ability of both groups being otherwise equal, the learning of B will interfere with the ability of Group II to recall what was learned in A. The difference between what is recalled by Group I and Group II is the degree of retroactive inhibition.

In our first equation, Group II will have a higher rate of recall. In the second equation, Group I will have the higher rate. The recall rate of both groups will be affected by the presence of a rest period in which no learning takes place.

Since almost every activity requires some type of learning, studies involving both forms of inhibition have required unusual precautions regarding the rest periods. If proactive inhibition can be reduced by limiting the amount of material to be learned, retroactive inhibition presents the greater problem to researchers. A Princeton University study shows the lengths to which scientists will go in their efforts to overcome this interference caused by activities taking place after learning.

Twenty students were selected as paid participants in a project designed to test the theory that some memory loss is due to the experiences we have following the learning period. The students were told they would not receive payment if they failed to follow all instructions accurately. Each was placed in a darkened chamber alone. After one minute of isolation, each was read a passage from Tolstoy's *War and Peace*. They were told to listen closely to the one hundred and eighty-two word passage, as they would be asked to repeat it verbatim.

When the passage was read, each student was asked to repeat it. Next, half the students were released and instructed to go about their normal activities. Before departing, they were asked to return in exactly twenty-four hours to conclude the project. The ten remaining were confined to beds placed in their chambers. Alongside each bed were food, water, and toilet facilities.

After twenty-four hours, the students who had been restricted to bed, totally isolated and undisturbed, were asked to repeat the Tolstoy passage. When the first group returned from the normal activities, each was placed in a chamber and also asked to repeat the passage. Not surprisingly, the students who remained in the chamber had a far greater ability to recall the passage than those who went about their normal activities.

The results confirmed the expectation that learning followed immediately by a period of diminished mental activity is retained much better than learning followed by normal mental activity.

Numerous additional studies have been done in which participants who were isolated after a learning session exhibited greater recall than when their learning was followed either by further instruction or normal daily activity. These consistent results prove that external stimulation interferes with the retention of previously learned material.

Since it's impossible for everyone to construct their own isolation chamber to enhance the learning environment, the quest began for a more practical means of reducing retroactive inhibition. The answer was sleep.

Learning, Memory, and Sleep

For years it was believed that the passage of time was responsible for memory loss. It was thought that material learned earlier simply faded or decayed. Ebbinghaus' memory curve disproved this concept. He found memory loss was most pronounced immediately after learning, and then the amount of loss tended to level off and the material retained remained constant. With the time-decays-memory theory in disrepute, the interference theory came into its own and still stands today. This is the proactive and retroactive inhibitions discussed earlier.

Dramatic support for this theory came from the Psychological Laboratory at Cornell University, when Dr. Karl M. Dallenbach conducted what became the classic study on interference and memory. The results showed "a marked difference in the rate of forgetting during sleep and waking."

Dallenbach's work proved that sleep helps considerably in remembering material learned, because no other learning takes place during sleep. Traditional daytime learning takes place before other activities, so it suffers from interference.

Although studies such as Dallenbach's demonstrated that retention of material learned was greater following several hours of sleep than normal daytime activity, several appeared to contradict their own results when the subjects were tested one hour after learning. When testing took place following one hour of sleep, the amount of material remembered was generally the same as after one hour of being awake. This raised an important question. If the reason for better retention during sleep is the absence of interference that normally occurs while we're awake, why are the results similar following one hour of being asleep and one hour of being awake?

The answer was given by Edward Van Ormer in the *Psychological Bulletin*. He suggested this was based on another activity, one that had yet to be examined. He said the first hour after learning is the most important for retention because there may be a process of consolidation that takes place before the actual memorizing. Assuming such an activity takes place during the first hour after learning, then the interference caused by being awake hinders that consolidation process. This same hindrance can occur to the person going to sleep after learning. This idea is best understood by breaking down into minutes that one hour between learning and being awakened for testing.

It takes the average person about ten minutes to fall asleep after learning. During those ten minutes, which may be the most important time for the consolidation process, the interference caused by waking activities or thoughts hinders the process. The very act of falling asleep may be an interference. Then, being awakened for testing probably causes additional interference. So, of the sixty minutes, at least the first ten are subject to interference inhibiting memorization. Add a few more minutes for the time it takes to fall asleep and we have a condition of negative memory.

During the next forty-five to fifty minutes, the memory process may be attempting to recoup what was lost during the first part of the hour. If being awakened causes interference, it will affect some of what we recouped. The time actually spent sleeping during that first hour may not be sufficient to offset what was lost through interference and achieve the improved level of memorization indicated by the test results following two or more hours of sleep. After two hours, results attained during sleep maintain an ever-widening superiority of recall over the same time spans of being awake.

Following these studies, numerous experiments have been conducted testing the relationship of sleep to memory. They've established conclusive proof that sleep has a positive affect on a person's ability to memorize information. This prompted some educators to question the efficacy of the conventional concept of students attending class during the early part of the day, followed by activities requiring additional learning.

Reviewing the theory of retroactive inhibition as a means of destroying the memorizing of learned material, and the role sleep plays in avoiding it, provokes the question most pertinent to this book: Is learning during sleep improved by the fact that there is no retroactive interference during the time the material is being processed into our memory?

While there have been no scientific studies on this specific question, we can draw some conclusions based on the work discussed in this chapter. That work supports the answer that learning during sleep will increase our ability to remember what is taught. Sleep learning enjoys some obvious advantages over traditional daytime learning methods. First, there's no interference while we're sleep learning. The environment in which we sleep is usually free of distractions that compete with learning. Second, if we're conscientious in preparing the sleep learning lesson, it will not be overloaded with too much information. Third, we've seen that repetition is a key to remembering. Repetition plays a major role in sleep learning. Fourth, we're learning during sleep, the great rest period that eliminates retroactive inhibition. Finally, when we're learning during sleep, our subconscious is a direct conduit to our memory.

4

The Mysterious Third
of Our Lives

What Sleep Is

In the previous chapter, we saw the relationship between learning, memory, and sleep. We now know the importance of sleep to the processing of information for memory storage. Most people assume sleep is a time of restfulness with little activity. This is hardly true. The major body systems continue to operate while we sleep, some at a higher rate than during waking hours. Of the three thousand calories burned each day by the average person, approximately eight hundred are burned off during an eight-hour sleep period. That's quite a lot of calories for a period of "little activity."

Sleep is a distinctly unique activity, different from all other human activities. Although the need for sleep varies as we progress from infancy to adulthood, the basic pattern of sleep remains the same. As we begin to fall asleep, certain physical changes occur within our bodies. Body temperature gradually lowers, muscles relax, and the amount of sugar being transported through the body declines. Perhaps the most readily identifiable symptom of sleep is the reduction of breathing rate. This is evident even before sleep actually occurs. The slowing of the respiration rate causes a reduction in the oxygen supply. Involuntary yawns provide additional oxygen.

These are the effects of sleep, but what is sleep and what function does it serve? The answers to these questions are most elusive. Miguel de Cervantes, the sixteenth-century Spanish novelist, called sleep the great equalizer for it "sets even, king and shepherd, fool and sage." Samuel Johnson agreed:

"Once in every twenty-four hours the gay and the gloomy, the witty and the dull, the clamorous and the silent, the busy and the idle, are all overpowered by the gentle tyrant and all lie down in the equality of sleep."

The questions surrounding sleep, what it is, why we do it, and what it does for or to us have always intrigued man. Sleep has been a subject of scientific research since research began.

Scientists are not the only ones interested in sleep. A visit to the paperback racks of any bookstore will provide ample evidence of the flood of interest people have in sleep, especially the incredible activity we call dreaming that takes place during sleep. The universal interest in sleep was demonstrated by the readers of the *Times* of London when that newspaper printed a questionnaire about people's sleep habits. Almost 25,000 readers responded.

Although the responses from the *Times*' readers revealed no difference in the length of time spent sleeping between men and women, they did support the belief that the amount of sleep-time required diminishes with age. While a teenager will spend an average of slightly more than nine hours each day sleeping, most adults require seven and one-half hours of sleep. Among those responding to the questionnaire, less than four percent said they slept an average of less than six hours, while one-third spent over eight hours a day sleeping. The remainder, almost two-thirds, reported sleeping between six and eight hours every night. A surprising revelation was that only slightly over one-half of the respondents felt that a night's sleep left them refreshed.

There was no difference between the sexes in required sleep-time, but there were some distinctions when it came to questions concerning dreaming. On the whole, women remembered dreams better than men, but men claimed to enjoy their dreams more. Women reported more nightmares, anxiety dreams, and almost twice as many dreams about the sea as men, while men reported more dreams about sex and money. Women dreamed more often in color.

Almost twenty-five percent of the respondents claimed they had experienced a dream prediction that had come true. Despite the fact, as we'll see later in this chapter, that science has established beyond a doubt that we may have six or more dreams during a single night's sleep, less than half the women and only one-third of the men said they dreamed more than once a night. The inability of most people to remember more than one dream a night supports the theory that memories of dreams last only about fifteen minutes unless they are particularly vivid.

Dr. William C. Dement, a leading authority on sleep research, feels sleep researchers have failed to define clearly the functions of sleep. Throughout the remainder of this book, the reader should keep in mind how little is known about sleep. For virtually every theory concerning sleep, an opposite theory exists. To confuse matters further, it's not uncommon for two researchers with opposing theories to present a separate series of studies and experiments supporting each respective position.

Dr. Ernst Schmidhofer, a neurophysiologist whose work with sleep learning as a therapy we'll discuss in a later chapter, put this situation of conflicting theories, each with its own documented proof, in perspective: "The side of the fence on which a given investigator finds himself is more likely to be determined by his personal feelings or by the way in which he sets up his experiments."

To fully understand how sleep learning works, which is essential to using it successfully, it is important to examine what is known about sleep. One misconception about sleep is that we move from an awakened state into light sleep, gradually slip into a deep sleep until we prepare to awaken, when we move back into a light sleep. Many researchers believed this until the mid-1950s, when several breakthroughs revealed the complexities of sleep.

It is now generally agreed that an entire sleep period is divided into two major states consisting of four to five separate phases. The two major states are vastly different from each other. One is an aggressive kind of sleep, while the other is a period of relative inactivity. Each is identified by several names. The terms most commonly applied to the active state are REM sleep (these initials denote rapid eye movements, one activity that takes place during this state), D-sleep (for desynchronized or dreaming), and paradoxical sleep. The less active state of sleep is known as non-REM sleep, S-sleep (synchronized), and orthodox sleep. For consistency and simplification, throughout this discussion we'll use REM and non-REM to denote the active and inactive states.

REM sleep is characterized by a great deal of activity besides the rapid eye movements for which it is named. The extraneous activity includes an increased or irregular pulse rate and elevated blood pressure. Conversely, non-REM sleep has an absence of rapid eye movements, low and steady pulse and respiration rates, and lower blood pressure. The amount of time spent in each state depends on the predisposition of the sleeper. Under what might be called "normal" conditions, such as having had a full sleep period the night before, non-REM sleep constitutes about seventy-five percent of the night. The remaining twenty-five percent of time is divided into a series of short REM episodes scattered throughout the night.

Two distinguished sleep researchers compared these changing states to the waxing and waning of ocean tides. The two states of sleep, they said, are like waves as they move in and out from the shore; they are not completely separate from each other, but there are temporary periods where one is dominant over the other. Just as a new ocean wave begins its approach to the beach before the previous wave completes its cycle, as each sleep state changes, one gradually overcomes the other until it is the dominant state.

The researchers claim that REM sleep is a state of readiness to receive incoming data. It is created by a process of "internally generated sensory input" that's reflected in dreaming. They see non-REM sleep as a response to an overloading of sensory and memory systems when there's too much incoming information. This explains why there is a concentration of non-REM during the early portion of sleep and a concentration of REM periods during later portions of sleep. If the appearance of non-REM sleep results from overloading due to high amounts of learning, then its concentration in the first few hours of sleep is in response to the amount of information that's been absorbed during the day.

This high concentration of non-REM sleep in the early portion of sleep is not found in animals or human infants. This may be caused by the fact both groups integrate their waking hours with short periods of sleep that reduce the intake of information and allow some of it to be processed during these periods. This habit of daytime napping by many mammals is credited as one reason for their survival during the prehistoric period of the earth's development. Despite the presence of extremely large and ferocious predator reptiles, smaller mammals were able to survive and continue their evolutionary development long after their enemies had vanished. Because these animals interspersed their days with periods of sleep, they were required to find and maintain secure hiding places, safe from their natural enemies. These sleep periods also permitted them to conserve their energy for finding food.

Many scientists believe REM sleep plays an active role in physical protection. They base this on the characteristic of REM sleep that brings the sleeper, humans included, to a condition of near waking and brief arousal that would allow a sensory sampling of the environment for possible danger. If danger is sensed, this near-waking condition, which exists only in REM sleep, prepares the sleeper for quick action, either fight or flight, as appropriate to the danger.

REM sleep is the state of sleep in which information processing takes place. Non-REM sleep is a reaction occurring when too much information is being processed. This can be interpreted as a rest period, after which the information processing resumes.

Earlier we saw that the amount of sleep a human requires decreases as adulthood is reached. There's also a change in the state in which much of that sleep is spent. During infancy and early childhood, a human will spend as much as fifty percent of sleep in REM sleep. As total sleep time declines with aging, most of that decline is composed of REM sleep. As much as seventy-five percent of REM sleep is lost in this way. The high concentration of REM sleep in early life is attributed to the greater volume of learning that takes place during these years. The amount of knowledge an infant or child learns, simply from daily experiences, is unmatched during any other time of life.

The characteristics of both REM and non-REM sleep continue to ebb and flow while we are awake. This may account for an otherwise unexplained phenomenon of human performance. Most measurements of speed and accuracy show a poor performance during the early hours of the day, with a gradual increase to a peak at midday. This is followed by a gradual decrease in performance to a low at bedtime. When we awaken, we are normally in REM, a state that continues in high concentration until about midday. At that time REM begins to recede, and non-REM gradually takes over. There are two basic conditions that can be attributed to REM sleep. The first, which we'll examine more closely, is the processing of information into memory. The second is a greater degree of alertness, which reveals itself in both speed and accuracy while we are awake.

The experts agree that we don't know enough about sleep to understand all its functions. It is clear, however, that during certain periods of sleep, information is processed into our memory. Other than that, we don't know why we sleep, except to say we must, for without sleep we cannot live. Sleep is itself self-regulating. Sleep patterns vary to some extent almost every night for each person, depending on the restorative requirements of the individual. Even strict monitoring with an EEG will invariably show inexplicable changes that are hard to explain by scientific means.

Why We Can't Live Without Sleep

Throughout history, sleep deprivation has been used to torture prisoners to extract information or confessions from them. Some modern examples of this are the interrogation methods used on American POWs during the Korean and Vietnam wars.

Psychiatric observation of several Air Force personnel who had given false confessions while held in North Korea revealed they were denied sleep. They were allowed only short naps from which they were awakened at irregular intervals for interrogation. Many of these men became disoriented and confused, and it grew increasingly difficult for most to distinguish between fantasy and reality. Some became temporarily psychotic. In this condition, they were easily susceptible to suggestion. Several were convinced by their captors they had been dropping germ-laden bombs on North Korea, even though they knew this to be untrue.

For those who are old enough to remember the trial of Josef Cardinal Mindszenty, will we ever be able to forget the pictures of the hollow-eyed, sometimes disoriented prisoner sitting in the mock courtroom? It was obvious even to the casual observer that he had been deprived of sleep in an attempt to force him to sign a false confession.

A New York City disc jockey named Peter Tripp gave us a famous example of the results of being deprived of sleep. Tripp conducted a "wakeathon" to raise money for the March of Dimes. It was announced that the disc jockey would stay awake for two hundred hours, making regular broadcasts from a glass-enclosed booth set up in Times Square.

Tripp actually remained awake for the full two hundred hours, during which he was observed by a team of medical doctors, psychologists, and other specialists. The first few days passed without incident, but as he approached the halfway mark, Tripp began to suffer visibly from the lack of sleep. He hallucinated cobwebs in his shoes, and a scientist's tweed suit turned into a pile of furry worms.

The last one hundred hours of his ordeal were the worst. After the fifth day, Tripp was taken to the Astor

Hotel to wash and change clothes, as had been done at regular intervals. Once inside the room, Tripp opened a bureau drawer, screamed, and fled. When they caught up with him, he told the doctors the drawer was on fire. A quick inspection found no trace of fire. Paranoia then set in. He accused the doctors of setting the fire to scare him. He then became convinced the same doctors were part of a conspiracy to put him in jail. At times he would back himself up to a wall, not permitting anyone to walk behind him.

As the final day of the "wakeathon" neared, Tripp began to question his own identity. The doctors found him constantly staring at the face of a clock mounted on the wall of the broadcast booth. When asked about this, he told them the clock's face had been transformed into the face of an actor friend of his, and he wasn't sure if he were really Peter Tripp or the actor.

On the last day, Tripp prepared for a pre-arranged examination by Dr. Harold Wolff, a renowned neurologist from Cornell University. The fact that Dr. Wolff dressed like an old-time undertaker, all black and formal, was the cause of the confused and disoriented disc jockey's final torment. As instructed, Tripp undressed and stretched out on the examining table set up for this purpose in a hotel room. As Dr. Wolf approached the table, Tripp, looking up at him, concluded that he was an undertaker and that the doctors were now conspiring to bury him alive. He immediately jumped from the table and headed for the door with the doctor and his associates in hot pursuit.

When the ordeal finally ended, Tripp slept for thirteen hours, after which he appeared physically recovered. He did, however, suffer a mild depression that lasted three months. Dr. Louis West, Chairman of Psychiatry at UCLA called his mental condition at the time "nocturnal psychosis." Dr. William Dement said: "The disc jockey developed an acute paranoid psychosis during the nighttime hours, accompanied at times by auditory hallucinations."

Despite his erratic behavior and mental state, Peter Tripp was able to broadcast his regular 5–8 P.M. radio show and do several "live" progress reports each day of his ordeal without revealing his "off the air" condition to his listeners.

There is much to learn about sleep, its function, and its relationship to our physical and mental condition. These are examples of the result of sleep loss and its accompanying behavioral changes. Sleep deprivation can be extremely dangerous, so most of the research done on this subject has been limited to animals. Experiments on dogs, cats, and rats have ended fatally for many of these animals when denied sleep for extended periods.

Sleep deprivation experiments using human subjects have demonstrated that physiological and chemical changes take place in the body, as well as behavioral changes. Researchers have found alterations in temperature, decrease in muscle strength, and changes in blood chemistry. From animal experiments, we know that prolonged periods of sleep loss have caused noticeable changes in brain tissue.

Removing sleep from man's life, even for short periods, may not have provided science with satisfactory answers about the function of sleep, but it has demonstrated how important it is to our well-being. Since the lack of sleep causes such dramatic mental confusion, it is obvious that during sleep our mind processes and clarifies information. Sleep learning takes full advantage of this function.

Dreams and Their Function

With few exceptions, most adults spend close to twenty-five percent of each night's sleep-time dreaming. However, their inability to remember dreams leads many to conclude they don't dream. This is a common misconception. In fact, little of what most of us dream is recalled the next morning.

Man has always dreamed, and has always assigned special importance to his dreams. In some ancient civilizations, dreams were used to forecast the future (these are called prediction dreams). Those individuals who correctly interpreted them—usually priests—were held in high esteem. Dreams, and the events taking place within them, were commonly an integral part of the religious practices of these societies. Often, dreams were thought to be the handiwork of evil spirits appearing in dreams disguised as humans. Early Asian civilizations believed that a person's spirit departed from the body during sleep and left the sleeper unprotected from these visiting demons.

The Greeks and Romans, both of whom built hundreds of temples for dream interpretation, placed all dreams into two categories. "Divine dreams" were those that had to be obeyed, while "ordinary dreams" did not. The Roman Emperor, Caesar Augustus, is reported to have walked the streets of Rome disguised as a beggar because he was instructed to do so in a "divine dream." Assyrian and Babylonian tablets dating back to 5,000 B.C. tell of the importance of dream interpretation to those civilizations.

Some cultures treated dreams as extensions of reality. Among Cherokee Indian tribes, a person reporting he was bitten by a snake in a dream was treated for a snakebite. An African tribal chief dreamed he had taken a trip to Britain. On awakening, he ordered a wardrobe of European-style clothes. When he donned them, his subjects congratulated him on his trip. The pharaohs of ancient Egypt relied on advice given by court dream interpreters. It's believed that guides for the interpretation of dream symbols were used in Egypt almost two thousand years before the birth of Christ.

The histories of most civilizations contain numerous instances of dream interpretations altering or creating important events. Hannibal made his march across the Alps because he had seen the fall of Rome in a dream. Julius Caesar marched on Rome because he dreamed he was sleeping with his mother, who symbolized the great city. The Moorish invasion of Spain took place because the leader of the Moors had a dream in which a prophet instructed him to do so.

Adolf Hitler credited a dream with saving his life during World War I. Asleep in a front-line trench, the future German dictator dreamed that he was buried alive under an avalanche of earth. When he awakened, Hitler was so upset he left the shelter and went for a walk. While he was away, the trench received a direct hit by enemy fire, its occupants buried alive. Imagine how different the world might be today had Hitler ignored that dream.

Religions always make extensive use of dreams. Mohammed is said to have received the mission of founding the Islamic religion, as well as complete details for its structure, in a series of dreams. The birth of Buddha was announced to his mother in a dream. According to Matthew, Joseph received instructions from an angel in three dreams: first to condone Mary's conception, then to take his wife and the child Jesus and flee to Egypt, and again, when Herod died, that it was safe to return to Israel.

The strong interest in dreams, dating back for centuries, continues today. Under various titles, dream interpreters ply their trade throughout many parts of the world. The continuing popularity among adults of Walt Disney's cartoon feature *Fantasia* is credited to its dream-like atmosphere. The film successfully captures the translatable symbols of dreaming by associating light colors and high musical notes with happiness, and dark colors and low notes with somber feelings. Many viewers of *Fantasia* describe its audio and visual effects as "experiencing a dream."

Sigmund Freud's symbolic interpretation of dreaming altered man's thinking on the subject, and superstition lost its grip on dream theories. The dream took on the role of a "guardian of sleep" and was believed to serve as a protection against disturbances that might awaken the sleeper. Some sleep researchers speculate that dreams, which always take place during REM sleep, are not really sleep at all, but a condition in which the sleeper is actually in a state almost identical to being awake.

When Freud said that dreams were related to human instinct, he was not espousing a new theory. Plato expressed much the same idea in *The Republic*: "In all of us, even in good men, there is a lawless wild beast nature, which peers out in sleep." Freud went further than Plato when he recognized that dreams often provide evidence of knowledge stored in our subconscious. He also said one component was common to all dreams: the repetition of an event from the previous day.

Research conducted since the 1960s provides substantial evidence that dreams have a definite role processing information into memories. A leading psychologist and dream therapist claims that the dreams are the by-product of a "physiological process connected to learning and remembering."

That dreams process information we have already absorbed is fascinating, especially when taken in context with learning while we sleep. Part of the basis behind this concept is that what we have learned must be processed into our long-term memories and assimilated into our past experiences. It is believed that everything we learn is processed through several levels to accomplish permanent long-term memory.

A noted psychiatrist and sleep researcher says we

should think of dreaming as two separate processes. The first is perception, which is a "working over" of information recently learned and collating it with experiences already in our memory storage. The second is "internal transformation," which he describes as the manipulation of previously stored information. The first process is where discrimination takes place and desired information is transferred from short-term to long-term memory.

The second process is a creative function. It can also be the root of fantasies and nightmares if the manipulation process fails to operate properly.

Not all events are relived in dreams. Several studies have shown that stressful or emotionally significant events occupy the greatest portion of our dreams. In one study, a group of people were shown a film containing emotionally charged material, while another group was shown the same film with this material edited out. The first group reported a much higher instance of dreaming about the film than the second group. One problem confronted by researchers is the failure to know all the dreams their subjects had. In this instance, it's possible that both groups dreamed about the film, but the first group recalled their dreams more vividly because of the inclusion of the emotionally charged material.

The residue of a day's experiences was recognized by Freud as an essential ingredient in the formation of dreams. Freud found that almost every dream incorporates a memory of, or allusion to, an event of the previous day.

If dreams are the means of processing information into our permanent memory, how then is this affected by sleep learning? The answer is simple yet surprising. It is possible for us to influence the content of our dreams and even control it to some degree. Before we discuss this, it is important that we understand how important dreams are to our lives, so we can better understand the role dreams play in learning, memory, and especially learning while we sleep.

The Importance of Dreams

Many people find it difficult to believe that everyone dreams several times each night. Since most people can normally recall only one dream a night, and some, no dreams at all most nights, they assume that dreaming is an irregular event that occurs only occasionally. Sleep researchers have conducted many studies of the consequences of preventing people from dreaming. Since dreams occur during REM periods of sleep, it is a simple matter to keep sleepers from dreaming by preventing them from entering REM sleep.

One study designed to prevent people from dreaming was conducted at a world famous New York City hospital. To keep the sleepers from dreaming, the researchers had to awaken each sleeper before the start of REM sleep. As the nights went by, the number of awakenings increased as the sleepers persisted in their efforts to enter REM sleep. The more the researchers deprived the sleepers of their dreams, the more determined were the sleeper's efforts to dream. Finally, one researcher complained that he was running back and forth to the bedroom so often that he could hardly keep up the pace.

This program ended on the fifth night with the discovery of "REM rebound," or the attempt to recover lost REM or dream periods. On the last night of testing, a sleeper who had normally averaged sixteen percent of the night in REM sleep vaulted to thirty-four percent REM time. Additional research revealed that people deprived of dreaming showed signs of anxiety, irritability, and increased difficulty concentrating.

Programs designed to curtail dreams mushroomed after

the one in New York. As the number of dreamless nights increased, the number of awakenings increased, and it became increasingly difficult to awaken the dreamless sleeper. By the time one weary volunteer reached his seventh night without REM sleep, he had to be awakened two hundred times. At this point, the researcher found the only way he could arouse his subject was to put cotton in his nostrils so he couldn't breathe.

In all dream deprivation experiments, EEG records were carefully maintained to make certain that sleepers did not enter REM sleep. Several researchers used separate control groups who were awakened the same number of times as the experimental group. This was a control measure to insure the results of the studies were based on loss of dream-producing sleep and not simply the result of too many awakenings during each night. These studies proved it is the loss of REM, or dream sleep specifically, that causes drastic alterations in a person's behavior, and not merely the loss of sleep itself.

As we have seen, people who are starved of dreaming suffer personality and behavioral changes, and as the number of dreamless hours increased these same people were increasingly more difficult to awaken. This indicates a vital need for dreaming.

In one typical incident, after the fifteenth consecutive dreamless night, the desire to dream had become so strong that the subject needed to be awakened thirty-six times in one hour to discourage dreaming. When this overwhelmed man was finally allowed to sleep, over sixty percent of his sleep time was absorbed by dreaming. This was nearly four times the amount of time he would normally spend dreaming before the experiment. Another subject of a similar experiment had shown psychotic characteristics while not being allowed to dream. When the experiment was completed and the subject was permitted to dream, he engaged in what may be the longest dream phase ever recorded: three hours of uninterrupted dreaming.

Mental function changes found in sleep-deprived people are usually traced to the absence of dreaming rather than loss of sleep. This was demonstrated by Peter Tripp, the New York disc jockey. The United States Public Health Service reported that Tripp's most severe periods of erratic behavior and hallucinations happened at those times when he would normally be dreaming, and continued for the average length of time of REM sleep.

The crucial changes that take place in people denied the time to dream suggest two conclusions. First, based on the relentless attempts to dream that increase rapidly with dream deprivation, it must be assumed that dreaming is an absolute necessity. Experiments on animals that resulted in death from prolonged denial of REM sleep have encouraged researchers to use extreme caution when working with human subjects. Tragically, an error by a researcher may one day give us conclusive evidence that dreaming is required to sustain human life.

The second conclusion concerns the function of dreams. As we've seen, being deprived of dreaming affects a person's personality and the ability to perform functions that require mental processes. This offers powerful evidence that vitally important mental functions are directly related to dreams.

The Laboratory Affect and Sleep Learning

The mechanisms that control sleep, and the functions sleep performs, are under constant examination in at least a dozen laboratories across the United States and countless more throughout the world. These laboratories are equipped with sophisticated apparatus for their research, including polygraphs, electroencephalographs, cardiographs, myographs, temperature meters, etc. It is here that psychologists, physiologists, biologists, psychiatrists, chemists, etc. are constantly learning more about the phenomenon called sleep.

The reliance on laboratory studies for knowledge about sleep has created its own distinct problem whose impact we cannot accurately measure. "Laboratory affect" is the term commonly used to describe alterations in normal sleep that occur when a person is sleeping in a controlled laboratory environment. These alterations are sharply visible for the first few nights as people adjust to sleeping in a strange environment while wearing a "headdress" of wires and electrodes.

After several nights, most sleepers usually make the necessary adjustment and begin transmitting information to the electronic instruments monitoring them. The need to use a laboratory environment and a "headdress" has always haunted researchers. Many question whether the data collected following the initial adjustment period is altered in some way by the laboratory affect. The question is especially troubling because it could have a profound effect on what we know about sleep.

The electroencephalograph (EEG) is one instrument used in the sleep laboratory. It is a polygraph which records the voltage fluctuations that occur between two points on a sleeper's scalp. A second instrument, the electroculogram (EOG), records a sleeper's eye movements. The cornea and retina of the eye each contain a different electrical potential and each movement of the eye causes a minute electrical change that can be measured and recorded. Still another device, the electromyogram (EMG), records the electrical changes that occur as a result of muscle activity.

A major function of the EEG is to provide researchers with the ability to determine the presence or absence of sleep. It also identifies for the researcher what state or phase of sleep the subject is in. The EEG operates on a simple principle. Like most medical electronic instruments, it measures changes in electrical potential. A measurement is made of the electrical current that "flows" from one point to another. Of the two electrodes stuck to a sleeping person's scalp, one point is "negative," another "positive." A comparison can be made between the electrical potential of a human head and that of a common automobile battery. If you placed a fully charged battery on a workbench, connected one end of an insulated cable to the positive (+) terminal, and passed the other end lightly over the negative (-) terminal, a spark would bridge the gap between the terminal and the cable. This spark is caused by the difference in electrical potential between the two terminals. If you placed a meter and recording device somewhere along the cable, you would be able to measure the current flow. The EEG does exactly that. The only difference is that the electrical potential between two points on a human scalp is altered by any of several physiological changes, including moving from one phase of sleep to another.

Entering a sleep laboratory is like entering a different world. A series of small, silver-colored discs are attached to selected areas of the sleeper's head and face. In preparation for this, each location to which an electrode will be attached must be thoroughly cleaned, usually with alcohol or acetone. The electrodes are "glued" on by a gel or a gauze pad soaked in collodin.

Each electrode is attached at a different point on the scalp or face. Each has a single, color-coded wire extending from its center. Usually eight of these discs will be attached, although the number can vary depending on the measurements to be recorded. The collection of brightly colored wires is then drawn through a wire harness near the top of the subject's head, forming what appears to be a multi-colored ponytail. When the subject settles into bed, the researcher connects each wire to an outlet on the wall above the bed. At the other end of the outlet, wires carry the current to the instrument center.

We can better appreciate the laboratory affect if we imagine for a moment what it must be like trying to get a normal night's sleep wearing this "headdress," while at the same time knowing someone will be watching and monitoring the electrical currents generated by your brainwaves. The laboratory affect is created by the attachments required to monitor sleep, the environment of the laboratory (even though most are made as homelike as possible), and the knowledge that someone is watching. How this alters the information being monitored is an unknown factor. How it affects a person's ability to perform functions that are a part of our sleeping capabilities is also unknown.

On an average night, two thousand feet of graph paper may be used to record sleep data from one individual. As the paper passes through the recorder, tiny pens responding to signals from the sleeping person move across the graph. Analyzing the results of an EEG reading is a laborious procedure. Every inch of the recording must be examined and interpreted.

As we'll see later, the laboratory affect may be the cause of much of the fence straddling that some researchers do on the subject of sleep learning. Most of the original experiments with sleep learning were done under laboratory conditions with more concern for proof that the subjects were asleep than for the learning experience.

Laboratory affect is the likely culprit that has prevented sleep learning from gaining wide scientific support and public acceptance in the United States. The Sleep Learning Association in Britain has overcome this obstacle, as have scientists in the Soviet Union, the nation that has done the most work with sleep learning. They've placed less emphasis on monitoring sleep and more on learning.

Their efforts have paid off with some remarkable results. If more researchers in the United States were concerned with proving the validity of sleep learning, instead of what frequently appears to be proving it doesn't work, perhaps millions of Americans would already have benefited from this learning technique.

Hypnosis, Sleep, and Learning

The successful use of sleep learning prompts many to assume a similarity between the states of hypnosis and sleep. This comparison is drawn primarily with "light sleep," when the subconscious is most receptive to suggestion. The most common period of "light sleep" is shortly after retiring or immediately before awakening, provided the time of awakening is pre-planned or regularly scheduled. The comparison of this stage of sleep with a hypnotic trance has been examined and tested with interesting results.

One significant investigation was conducted by a psychologist who was a research fellow at the National Institute of Mental Health. The project involved twenty-two people who had volunteered for what was described as a study in which they would be given a psychological test while they slept. Each volunteer slept in a separate room. During the night, the psychologist entered each sleeper's room and whispered a command into the ear of each volunteer. His command was "clasp your hands together." In each instance, the sleeping person clasped both hands together within ten seconds of the order. Following that response, he again whispered another command to each sleeper. This time he said, "Your hands are hard . . . solid . . . completely interlocked . . . it is impossible to unclasp your hands." Keep in mind that the volunteer's hands were still clasped together as directed in the first command.

The psychologist repeated the last command continuously for one minute. Finally he added "Try it!" The sleepers obeyed the order and all tried without success to pull their hands apart. To further confirm their susceptibility, the volunteers then underwent seven standard tests to evaluate the suggestibility levels of persons under hypnosis. All were still in natural sleep. The test consisted of additional commands from the psychologist. "You are becoming very thirsty and will wake up in exactly five minutes and drink lots of water. You cannot open your clenched fist. Your fingers are rising. Your hand is dead and dull and numb and you can't feel anything at all. When you awaken you cannot remember anything I said."

Three of the twenty-two participants awoke during the tests. Although not completely awake, seven others either opened their eyes momentarily or moved, indications that the tests disturbed their sleep. The twelve remaining sleepers gave no indication of disturbed sleep. All measurements, including breathing rate and movement, were normal.

Using the widely accepted Davis and Husband scale for the measurement of the depth to which a person is hypnotized, the results of the suggestibility tests on the twelve volunteers who remained in undisturbed sleep showed that if they had been under hypnosis instead of in natural sleep, they would have been in the third or deepest stage. On awakening, the subjects responded to the commands given them while asleep as if they were responding to post-hypnotic suggestions. Most required several glasses of water to quench an unusually strong thirst and had difficulty unclasping their hands.

To further evaluate the results, the twelve subjects who remained asleep during the suggestibility test were put through a standard hypnotic-induction procedure. The average score of the volunteers showed "no significant difference" between their responses when they were asleep and when they were under hypnosis. In fact, the scores produced by the subjects while asleep were actually higher than when they were hypnotized. This meant that the volunteers were more open to suggestion when they were lightly sleeping than when they were hypnotized.

The similarity of being receptive to suggestion while under hypnosis and while in natural sleep opened a promising new application for sleep learning: conditioning for self-improvement. If most people are as receptive during sleep as under hypnosis, then it is possible the therapeutic techniques administered through clinical hypnosis can also be used on sleeping subjects.

The use of hypnotic suggestion to achieve such goals as improved study habits is well known to both psychologists and educators. One program involved a group of forty-nine schoolchildren who were attending a five-week reading clinic. Nine of the children were placed under hypnosis and given suggestions aimed at increasing their motivation and interest in reading and improving their attention and concentration. Tests conducted before and after the reading clinic proved that the students who received hypnotic suggestions "performed significantly better than those who did not."

Hypnotic suggestion has been used for years to reduce pain and has received serious attention from behavioral therapists. This is an area requiring a separate study, but the point is valid that the self-improvement, or character building, that can be accomplished as a form of conditioning through hypnosis is also possible through self-administered sleep learning. In fact, a popular coed at a large Northeastern university, more inclined to a full social life instead of academic pursuits, used a combination of sleep learning and self-hypnosis to change her habits. The result was that she raised her grade average by more than one full point.

5

How Sleep Learning Works

The Foundation of Sleep Learning

We have now reviewed the three major human components related to sleep learning: the subconscious mind, the process of learning and memorizing, and sleep. Before proceeding, let us assemble and summarize the most relevant facts from the previous chapters. They will serve as a foundation on which to build a successful sleep learning program. Then we will examine how sleep learning will work for you, and look at successful examples of sleep learning.

Fact 1. Information channeled into our memory through our subconscious remains with us indefinitely.

Fact 2. In a state of deep relaxation, the discriminatory power of our conscious mind is greatly reduced.

Fact 3. While we're asleep, that roadblock is reduced even further.

Fact 4. Activity during the latter part of the day interferes with memorizing what had been learned earlier in the day.

Fact 5.   This interference does not take place during normal sleep.

Fact 6.   Repetition is a major key to memorization.

Fact 7.   REM sleep is the time that learned information is processed into our memory.

Fact 8.   Susceptibility to suggestion while in deep relaxation and light sleep is similar to being under hypnosis.

When we learn while we sleep, we avoid the roadblocks erected by the conscious mind (Facts 2 and 3) and channel our lessons through our subconscious (Fact 1) where they are better retained. Learning while asleep eliminates the problems of interference or distraction from the learning process (Facts 4 and 5). Memorization is aided by the reliance on repetition of the sleep lessons (Fact 6). When we learn while asleep, we're learning at what may well be the best time, when information is being processed (Fact 7) and when we are receptive to the lessons, (Fact 8).

To consolidate these facts into one sentence: Sleep is the best time to learn because of the absence of interference, the availability of the subconscious mind, and the information processing function sleep serves.

The facts we've established in the preceding chapters now raise the important question, "Can we really hear clearly while we sleep?" It will surprise those who continue to insist that sleep is a period of mental inactivity, but not only can we hear while we sleep, we can also discriminate between important and unimportant sounds. More importantly, we have the ability to react, even physically, to what we hear.

Listening While We Sleep

Scientific method has validated the efficacy of sleep learning. In this chapter, and those that follow, we will review the evidence and compare it with some of the numerous practical uses of sleep learning.

There is a substantial body of evidence concerning our ability to hear and relate to things while asleep. This is, of course, a key to sleep learning. This evidence comes not only from scientific research such as laboratory experiments, but also from the actual everyday experiences of most people. A humorous example is that of the snoring professor who developed the habit of falling asleep while attending meetings and conferences. Although a speaker at one of these meetings might be insulted to find him sound asleep in the middle of a presentation, the good professor made matters even worse. He snored, loudly! Not only would he fall asleep in the middle of a speech, but he provided competition for the speaker through his persistent snoring.

To the great surprise of others in the audience, the professor would often suddenly stop snoring, come fully awake, and correct some minute error made by the speaker. This became a disconcerting aspect of the mathematician's personality and provoked one of his colleagues to remark: "He'd snore in your face as you talked, but if you made a mistake he would wake up and correct you."

Another example of man's ability to hear and absorb information while in deep relaxation and sleep comes from Dr. Anthony R. Ruffino. Dr. Ruffino's experience occurred while a student at the Dental College of New York University. It is an experience not unfamiliar to many, especially those who attended schools of higher learning where the practice of "cramming" for an important examination is part of a student's life.

"While studying for an anatomy exam which was part of the freshman year of dental school, my friend Artie and I decided that we would need the whole night to study in order to be adequately prepared. Staying up all night was certainly not unknown to us, for the normal rate of "plugging" often demands it. But on this night, having recently completed several other exams, we were really too tired to endure the whole night; at least I was— Artie was more accustomed to these marathon sessions.

"Toward about 4 A.M., when we were covering subjects like the detailed anatomy of the middle ear, and the course and distribution of the seventh cranial nerve, I found myself in a stupor that was very much akin to sleep. Artie continued to read, and when he asked me a question I was not awake enough to respond. After several hours of the routine of sleeping for a few minutes alternating with periods in which I was more asleep than awake, I remember being able to hear Artie's voice but sensing a great confusion regarding what he was telling me. Several times he repeated mnemonic devices to aid in the remembering of certain progressions of anatomic facts. Finally, I fell dead asleep and was awakened by Artie at 7 A.M. with just enough time to get to school for the exam. The results of that night's studying still amaze me. Although I felt, at the time I was awakened, that I was confused and did not have command of the topics covered during my stupor, I did very well on the exam and several questions that I gave correct answers for were topics that I had no conscious memory of having studied. The test was comprised of fifty questions, and I would guess that at least fifteen of the answers came from some semi-conscious source, most probably the retention of Artie's words even though I was asleep."

A strikingly similar experience was reported by Professor A. M. Svyadoshch. Answering a questionnaire circulated by the professor, a neuropathologist wrote that she experienced what she called "incidental learning" while studying for an exam with a group of classmates. While one of them was reading aloud, the woman fell asleep. When she awoke, she was able to recall everything that was read while she slept.

Further evidence comes to us from a less obvious source, the anesthetized patient. Anesthesia not only causes loss of pain sensation, but can also induce a state of unconsciousness similar to sleep. In her book *The Brain Changers*, Maya Pines relates an incident involving a woman anesthetized for a hysterectomy operation. During a post-operative visit, the surgeon detected a distinct coolness in her attitude. It was obvious the patient was angry with him. It turned out that during the operation, while the patient was "asleep," the doctor made the comment, "Well, that takes care of this old bag." To the surgeon's chagrin, the patient heard him and, despite his protestations that he was not referring to her but to the organ he had just removed, the woman never forgave him.

We know we respond with voluntary and involuntary reactions to external stimulation while awake. We experience such stimulation through our senses, by seeing, hearing, smelling, or touching. Our reactions are sometimes instinctive, while other times we're required to consider possible reactions, select one, and make a voluntary response to the stimulation. A response can take numerous forms. The type of response with which we are concerned here is that which causes the formation of mental images or visualizations. By comparing our visualization response to outside influences, both while awake and asleep, we will understand more clearly the fallacy of a popular misconception about sleep.

Many people believe their mental functions require rest periods much like their physical need for rest. How often have we heard a person say, "I can't study anymore,

I'm too tired, my mind won't function properly,'' or, ''My mind needs a rest,'' or, ''My brain is too tired''? References to the mind and brain are intended for the mental processes we associate with them. As we saw in the previous chapter, the mind's processes continue to function twenty-four hours a day, regardless of whether we're awake or asleep.

Mental images can be formed under myriad circumstances. If we have a telephone conversation with someone we've never met, it's natural for us to try to develop a ''mental picture'' of what we think that person may look like, try to give the voice a face. When we do this, we're creating a visualization response (the mental picture) to an external stimulation (the person's voice). The same thing happens while we sleep.

A similar reaction to verbal stimulation is triggered when we hear a key word or phrase that arouses our memory. To understand how this happens, let's assume a hypothetical situation in which you've just met an old friend who recently returned from a distant city you also visited several years ago. Your friend tells you about his trip and, as the conversation develops, he mentions several places that you also had visited. The names of these locations are trigger words to which you react with a visualization. One trigger word is the name of a famous monument. Immediately your mind begins to search its data bank. Presently the correct image is retrieved and your response to the mention of the monument is a ''mental picture'' of the monument as you saw it several years earlier. Such responses can be based on actual knowledge, such as in this example, or can be created by imagination or assumptions, such as relating an image of how we visualize how people look based on the sound of their voice on the telephone. A novelist creates ''mental pictures'' in the minds of readers by supplying just the right amount of information about a character or location to engender a visualization response.

Despite persistent "mind needs rest" comments, our reactions to external stimuli continue while we sleep. A common example is the sleeping person who brushes away a fly that's landed on his cheek. It is an involuntary reaction that produces a physical movement. Another common example demonstrating that our mental functions operate while we sleep is the reaction of a mother to her crying child. She may be a sound sleeper who is rarely disturbed by sounds in the night, but the moment her child begins to cry she wakes up. Not only are the mother's mental functions alert while she sleeps, they are capable of discriminating between unimportant sounds and those of great importance where her child is concerned. A sound such as her baby's cry requires her to awaken, so she does.

Physical responses such as chasing away a fly or waking aren't the only reactions of which we are capable during sleep. Even more significant to our examination of sleep learning is the visualization reaction that occurs during sleep. Realizing that this occurs and understanding its importance to the memory process gives us a better appreciation of how sleep learning works.

Freud believed that visualized responses to sounds we hear while asleep can be incorporated into our dreams, which are, after all, mental images themselves. He cited an incident that took place in 1865. While asleep, a person received an unusual external stimulation when a bedpost fell across his neck. His reaction was transformed into a dream in which he was guillotined during the French Revolution. Hundreds of experiments conducted since then support Freud's theory and extend it further. They show that even a person's name spoken to him while he sleeps can cause a visualization response that could be included in his dreams.

During the past twenty years there have been dozens of professionally controlled programs dealing with the ability of humans to hear while they sleep. A continued review of these experiments would be redundant. It is more beneficial to learn how to use the information we absorb during sleep. The studies done in this area are sufficient proof that sleeping people are capable of hearing what is said to them. These same studies also prove that not only can we hear while we sleep, but we also comprehend the meaning of what is said.

Reacting to What We Hear

Knowing that we can hear and understand what is said while we sleep prompts the question of whether what we hear actually has any real meaning for us.

Many people have trained their subconscious to ignore familiar or routine sounds that occur while they sleep. People who live close to a railroad track do this to avoid having their sleep disturbed by passing trains. Yet the same person will quickly awaken at the unfamiliar sound of screeching automobile tires, even though the train noise may be louder.

Evaluating the sounds or information we hear during sleep isn't limited to those sounds which are distinctly meaningful or meaningless. This was demonstrated by the snoring professor who slept through the presentation at a conference, awakening only to correct what he felt was an error.

Sleepers who awaken at the sound of a specific stimulus, such as the cry of a child, or the incorrect statement, have successfully taught themselves to respond in this manner. For the mother, it is her desire to care for the infant. For the professor, it is the need to correct an erroneous statement. Because of this, the sleep learner who is highly motivated to learn the material can be assured of success.

In fact, from the examples we've discussed it's clear that most people have already experienced the phenomenon of hearing something while asleep, evaluating its significance or meaning, and, when necessary, responding to what was heard. It's possible this happens to each of us nightly without our being conscious of it. The occasions that we are able to recall are those that provoke a physical response, such as awakening. Our goal is to make productive use of this inherent natural ability. Once we've done this, we'll be able to expand our knowledge and our lives.

Learning While Asleep

There is no doubt we have the ability to hear while we sleep. There is also no doubt we have the capacity to evaluate what we hear while asleep. This was clarified by the findings of two doctors who conducted extensive sleep studies under a grant from the United States Public Health Service. They concluded that the ability of man to discriminate between sounds heard while asleep is "general knowledge."

If we could not hear and respond, it would be impossible for us to learn during sleep. The question is: "Can real learning take place during sleep?" The preponderance of information available from psychological studies alone makes the answer abundantly clear: Yes, we can learn while asleep. The scientific approach to sleep learning has been conducted with two major uses in mind. First, sleep learning can exist separate and independent of other learning. Second, sleep learning can be used as an aid to increase or reinforce traditional daytime learning.

Dr. William H. Johnson examined the second use in his work. Dr. Johnson conducted an investigation of sleep learning that prompted him to conclude: "... that hearing material during sleep can facilitate learning the same material in the waking state."

Johnson used eight young men in his study, paying each $45 for participating. As a way of creating motivation, Johnson said he would pay an additional $15 to each of his subjects who successfully passed a test of his recall of what he learned while asleep. Volunteers were selected based on their responses that they: (1) were moderately good to very good sleepers; (2) fell asleep quickly after going to bed; (3)were awakened only by an average to loud sound; (4) generally fell back to sleep quickly after being awakened; (5) functioned well shortly after awakening; and (6) had absolutely no knowledge of the Russian language.

The volunteers spent eight consecutive nights in Dr. Johnson's laboratory. Each night while they slept, they were presented with either the experimental material, Russian words and their English translations, or control material consisting of pairs of random numbers. During half the nights this was presented while they were in REM sleep, and the other half during non-REM sleep. To assure they were asleep, accurate recording by EEG was maintained whenever material was presented. Following the presentation of material, each man was awakened and tested for what he had learned.

As each man arrived at the lab, he was instructed to routinely prepare for bed. When they were in bed, the following taped message was played to each:

> "You know that your ability to learn while you are asleep depends entirely on your willingness to cooperate. Because if you don't want to learn while you are asleep, we won't be able to make you do it. But if

you pay close attention to what I say and follow what I tell you to do, it will be very easy for you to learn to fall into a very deep sleep and you will learn. We are confident of your ability to learn while you are asleep, but you must relax and now go to sleep. . . . Pay careful attention to what I will say and you will go to sleep very soon. You will go into a very deep sleep and you will learn Russian.''

Shortly after each participant had fallen asleep, he heard another message:

"This is your Russian teacher. You can hear my voice but you will not wake up. You are asleep and relaxed and you can hear my voice. And you will not wake up. Presently you will hear Russian words and their English meanings. You will hear them clearly but you will not wake up. Listen to them and commit them to memory. Memorize them completely. Learn them tightly, firmly. You will remember these words and their meanings forever.''

Following a few more instructions not to awaken and to memorize the material, the lesson began. There were twelve repetitions of a list of ten Russian/English words each night for a total of one hundred twenty combinations. Each nightly lesson lasted approximately one hour.

As each man was awakened, the electrodes were removed from his head and his ability to recall the lesson and to relearn the material was tested. The fact that the subjects were awakened too soon after the presentation of the lessons contributed to the low scores obtained, although the results did lead Dr. Johnson to say, "... subjects scored higher on the nights upon which they first heard the material to be learned during sleep than when they had not heard the material.''

Doctors Clarence Leuba and Dorothy Bateman conducted another investigation of sleep learning. Their subject was Mrs. B., who claimed she could recall information that had been broadcast over the radio while she was sleeping. Mr. B. was in the habit of listening to the radio while his wife slept.

A phonograph was placed in Mrs. B.'s bedroom. Over nine consecutive nights, three different songs, were played, one song for each three-night period. The phonograph was connected to an automatic timer that turned it on during the night, allowed the song to play five times, then shut it off. Following each three night period, Mrs. B. was tested for her knowledge of the song. The first song was recalled with three minor errors, but the second and third were recalled perfectly. Mrs. B. had no prior knowledge of the three songs used.

In a sleep learning program conducted at Duke University, forty students were divided into two groups. Before the study began, two recordings were made, each containing fifteen three-letter words. Each recording had a different list, and each list was repeated five times.

Before sleeping in the laboratory, all forty men were taught the list from one recording. Each was tested and scored on a basis of how many times the list had to be played before he could anticipate all fourteen words after being told the first. The average scores for both groups were similar, which permitted the assumption that they could be considered equal in learning ability for this type of material.

The second recording of fifteen words was played for only one group while its members slept. The following morning, both groups were taught the second list of words and tested on it as they were on the first list. The group that heard this list while they slept had a significantly better ability to master this list than the other group. The researcher concluded that, ''The evidence obtained suggests that there is retention of auditory material presented during sleep."

Doctors Martha Koukkou and D. Lehmann conducted sleep learning experiments on a total of twenty-one volunteers in both Athens, Greece, and San Francisco. Using a recall test procedure, they confirmed the successful teaching of sentences of their sleeping subjects.

Two New York City psychologists taught a list of paired associates to several sleeping undergraduates. Paired associates are two words the subject learns as a set. Successful learning is tested by giving the first word in each set and having the subject respond with the matching word.

During each of three nights, the list was presented seventeen times. The work was done in a laboratory and the material presented only during non-REM sleep periods. The results prompted the researchers to conclude: "Clearly, pre-presentation of a list of meaningful paired associates during the non-REM stages of sleep benefits subsequent learning of that list."

There have been numerous similar studies of sleep learning. The results of all this work provide indisputable evidence of our ability to learn while we sleep. This was substantiated by Dr. Laverne C. Johnson of the United States Navy Medical Neuropsychiatric Research Unit. In summarizing a review of the subject, Dr. Johnson said: "Information processing during sleep is summarized, and published reports lead to the conclusion that the sleeping brain does receive, process and perhaps even store information presented during sleep."

An extensive review of the scientific work done on sleep learning was conducted by Dr. Louis Aarons of the Illinois Department of Mental Health and Developmental Disabilities. In the review, titled *Sleep-Assisted Instruction*, Dr. Aarons points out the different emphasis in experimental methods used in the Soviet Union and the

United States. Where measuring sleep has been a major concern in the United States, the Soviets ''have been more concerned with stimulus properties, suggestibility, set and training in hypnopaedia.'' He questioned the extensive use of EEG monitoring in the United States. ''The selection of EEG recordings to define sleep may unduly limit opportunities for the phenomenon of sleep learning.''

Soviet studies also differ from American in the type of material used for sleep learning. Most programs conducted by Soviet and other European scientists make use of material that is meaningful to the participants. This results in good motivation and attention. Many American programs have relied on getting the sleeper's attention through such devices as buzzers. There have also been too many American experiments using meaningless material. This must have a negative effect on the motivation of the subjects of these programs.

Successful sleep learning programs rely on both repetition and a longer period of time for the subject to absorb the material. They also require preparation that can consist of simply reading or listening to the material to be learned before going to sleep, or a pre-sleep message such as the one used by Dr. Johnson when he taught students Russian words.

William H. Emmons and Charles W. Simon conducted experiments and wrote several articles on sleep learning. Critics of sleep learning have relied heavily on their results. In evaluating these experiments, their methods and motives appear questionable. In one experiment, twenty-one men were bombarded with ninety-six questions and corresponding answers while they slept. The next morning they were asked the same questions and expected to provide the correct answers. Emmons and Simon stated unequivocally: ''Learning during sleep is concluded to be impractical and probably impossible.''

These researchers overlooked one overwhelmingly important fact: Repetition is as important to sleep learning as it is to learning while awake. In his book *Memory*, Professor of Psychology Ian Hunter said:

> "There is no question about the importance of repetition in memorizing. When information is received and must be retained for use in a short time hence, the retaining appears to be accomplished by some sort of repetitive rehearsal of the information."

The absence of repetition is a common thread that runs through unsuccessful sleep learning programs. Another is the inconsequential nature of the material presented to the sleepers. They run the gamut of random numbers, one-syllable nouns, nonsense words, irrelevant statements, and other assorted disjointed and meaningless information that failed to contribute to the sleepers' motivation to learn.

This raises a serious question concerning a possible difference in how we recall various types of material. Meaningful material is more easily remembered than is unimportant information.

Frequently, researchers attempt to force-feed inane information to subjects who have absolutely no motivation to learn the material. This deficiency is emphasized when we consider the guidelines used by Professor L. A. Bliznitchenko, who has successfully used sleep learning under scientifically approved conditions. Speaking of the basic requirements for successful sleep learning, he tells us:

> "Thus, 'desire' (to learn the material being presented), 'tuning in' (psychologically) and the 'arrangement' (how the material is presented—tone of

voice, repetition, etc.) has great significance in hypnopaedia (sleep learning)."

On the subject of repetition, Professor Bliznitchenko states emphatically ". . . multiple repetition is obligatory in all cases (of sleep learning)."

Dr. William C. Dement, whom we discussed earlier, took Emmons and Simon to task for their methodology.

"It should be noted, however, that in one test these experimenters used complex questions and answers and presented each pair only once; in another test they used nonsense material. Some of the complex material might have been learned if it had been presented repeatedly. The nonsense material may have been discarded because it had no relevance for the sleeping subjects."

The evidence is conclusive: Sleep learning is an effective way to learn for many people. We know that certain criteria must be met if sleep learning is to be used successfully. These include motivation to learn and repetition of the material. In the following two chapters, we'll turn our attention to two areas in which sleep learning has been used successfully: the learning of a foreign language and as an aid in therapy. Before moving on, we'll take a look at a collateral area of the overall subject of sleep learning, learning while in deep relaxation.

Relaxation Learning

The question is often raised: "If the subconscious is receptive to suggestion during sleep, is it equally receptive during the pre-sleep relaxation which so closely approximates light sleep?" The beginnings of an answer started to be formulated in the mid–1960s, when two professors at the University of Sverdlovsk began experimenting with what they called the "sleeping method" of learning.

Their early experiments proved so successful that Professor of Psychology Ratmir S. Orlov and Professor of Foreign Languages V. Repin were encouraged to state: ". . . a person in a state of relaxation possesses the same enhanced ability in memorizing as a person learning in his sleep following the method of hypnopaedia."

Pre-sleep and post-sleep relaxation are the conditions experienced either just preceding or following sleep. Because these conditions are similar, we'll concentrate on pre-sleep relaxation only. As an individual progresses through pre-sleep relaxation, alertness begins to wane from wakefulness to relaxation and, finally, to the sleep states.

Proponents of learning during relaxation claim the presence of both early sleep and the gradual decline of alertness combine to achieve an enhanced suggestibility level. Because receptiveness is enhanced by alertness, the state of relaxation offers a prime period for learning and memorizing.

Assembling student volunteers with a desire to learn English, Repin and Orlov used English words in two projects. The first used pre-sleep relaxation. While the students were in this state, fifty unfamiliar English words were read to them through a tape recorder several times over for twenty minutes. When they were awakened, the students were asked what they remembered. They recalled an average of forty-one to forty-four words, or approximately eighty-five percent of the material. They were then given five minutes to rehearse the newly learned words. When they were tested a second time, their memorization improved to an average of ninety-five percent of the words.

Later, this same group spent two to three hours memorizing fifty different English words. Although the results varied widely, with some recalling all the words in this second list and others able to recall less than half, collectively they learned only seventy to eighty percent of the words. The results during relaxation proved far more successful in the memorizing of foreign words than did the traditional method.

With no advance warning, the students were re-tested three months later. They demonstrated a marked decline in the number of words recalled from the list they learned while awake. This time their recall average dropped to fifty to sixty percent of that list. In contrast, they remembered a much higher percentage of the words they learned while in a state of relaxation. The recall rate dropped only a few percentiles from ninety-two to ninety-eight percent to an average of ninety to ninety-four percent. A factor contributing to both declining rates is the lack of practical use during the intervening period.

Repin and Orlov tested these results in a second program, this time doubling the word groups to one hundred English words each. The students learned one group while in relaxation, the other while awake, just as in the earlier experiment. After a six-month interval the retention of words was exceedingly low in both categories. The researchers concluded that one hundred words of a foreign language were too many to learn and memorize successfully in a short period. A study of the ability of the students in the first group to memorize the material showed that the words learned during relaxation were retained thirty to fifty percent more accurately than those learned while awake.

In still another program, Repin and Orlov attempted to teach forty foreign words and phrases to students who were in pre-sleep deep relaxation. During the fifteen-minute lessons, the students were able to memorize an average of ninety to ninety-five percent of the material.

In yet another study, a group of students in pre-sleep relaxation received a special suggestion instructing them to memorize the foreign words they would be taught during the next twenty minutes. The addition of a suggestion to memorize improved the students' ability to commit the words to memory. Without the suggestion they could recall eighty-three percent of the words. Following the suggestion they recalled almost eighty-nine percent. This proved that the ability of our subconscious to memorize information is enhanced by the simple suggestion that we do so.

Professor Repin reports that he and his associates were "astonished" by the results they obtained when they used relaxation learning to help students overcome nervous tension before taking exams or participating in important sports events.

The Soviets aren't alone in recognizing the potential of the deep relaxation state. Similar programs have been conducted in the United States by Thomas Budzynski, an electrical engineer with a Ph.D. in psychology. Dr. Budzynski is Clinical Director of the Biofeedback Institute of Denver, and an assistant clinical professor in the Department of Psychiatry at the University of Colorado Medical Center. He describes what he calls the "twilight state" (deep relaxation) as a period when people "are hyper-suggestible and capable of learning certain things more efficiently and painlessly than during the day. . . ."

Budzynski discovered a means of solving the major difficulty with relaxation learning: i.e., the short time people are in this state. Usually we either quickly gain consciousness and awaken, or fall asleep. Budzynski overcame this with the Twilight Learner, a device developed by him and an another engineer. It helps maintain the presence of theta brain waves during learning activity. According to Budzynski, theta waves are present only during the twilight period. Using biofeedback, Dr. Budzynski and his colleagues have trained people to maintain the relaxation state. The Twilight Learner accomplishes two goals: It warns a properly trained person when he or she is slipping out of the twilight state, and it supplies the audio messages for learning.

Electrodes placed on the scalp of a twilight learning student pick up and transmit the student's brain waves to the recorder. If those waves are theta, the lesson is played on a cassette recorder. If the student's brain waves change to alpha waves, indicating increased alertness, the lesson stops playing. Should the frequency of the theta waves alter, indicating the onset of sleep, the volume of the lesson increases, bringing the student back to the twilight state.

Budzynski used his Twilight Learner to help a student who had previously failed an examination for a Spanish language course. The student was so anxious about failing the exam a second time that he was having difficulty studying. A tape recording was prepared containing positive suggestions that the student would be able to concentrate and remember the Spanish/English material that followed. During the twilight state, the student heard the tape twelve times. He was then able to study effectively and passed the exam.

The Twilight Learner has also been used to overcome "mental blocks" such as those developed by overweight people against dieting. A man who could not be assertive enough to say "no" had a "dramatic improvement" after five weekly sessions of twilight learning. Budzynski also reports successful results using twilight learning to solve problems with insomnia and alcohol abuse.

Twilight or relaxation learning has received considerable attention in other areas. A researcher at Pepperdine University used it to successfully teach 1,800 foreign words to students in 120 hours. Bulgaria's Georgi Lozanov combined a recorded message with background music for relaxation learning or "suggestopedia," as he calls it.

Whether it's called relaxation learning, twilight learning, or suggestopedia, learning while in deep relaxation has a promising future. The day has come when relaxation and sleep are not considered "wasted time." With this recognition, revolutionary new techniques in the educational process may not be far behind.

Sleep Learning Around the World

Sleep learning has attracted the interest of investigators in many countries. The work being done in the field, both scientific and non-scientific, has not yet been coordinated sufficiently to establish a uniform approach to programming sleep learning research. A first step in accomplishing this was the creation of the Sleep Learning Association in England. This group has been responsible for several publications dealing with scientific research. One major accomplishment of the Association was to establish channels of communications between sleep learning researchers in Western Europe and their counterparts in Eastern Europe.

A similar organization was formed in Prague, Czechoslovakia. Under the direction of Professor Cenek Heinz, the Suggestive Hypnopaedia Group conducted a series of experiments summed up in the following comment from Heinz: "Knowledge of the English language can be imparted to students whose intelligence is about the average and who have no previous knowledge of English, within 8 to 10 days. With intensified daytime teaching and intensified hypnopaedia tuition (nocturnal lessons), we have achieved those standards of knowledge of English which are produced by school courses extending over three years."

One course conducted by Professor Heinz and his associates was sponsored by the Institute of Further Education and the Ministry of Chemical Technology. The subject again was English, and the course combined daytime with nocturnal instructions and consisted of twelve lessons. Here are some comments made by several students who participated in this course.

"One can say with certainty that the effect of this teaching method is of greater magnitude than the classical method." Jaroslav Civin, B.Sc.

"The great difference between this method and that used hitherto, as I know it, became apparent in the first couple of days." A. Hruby, B.Sc.

"I consider this a very original and dynamic method. Even after this short time, the student is saturated with the essence of the English language, which gives the impression that he has been taught much longer than is fact." Milan Vlacil

"I consider this the only usable system for teaching languages to overworked personnel." S. Razl

There have been other foreign language sleep learning programs in Czechoslovakia, attended by government officials from various agencies throughout the country, including the Department of Foreign Trade in Liberec, Northern Bohemia; the Director of the Administration of Home Trade Training Institutes, Prague; the Economic University at Bratislava, Slovakia; the Slovakia Scientific Trade Institute; the Director of the National Rubber Company, Central Bohemia; the Director of the Training Institute of the Ministry for the Chemical Industry, and the Director of the Slovakian Shipyards. Most of these officials participated in sleep learning courses to learn English.

In Budapest, Hungary, a student named Kohalmir con-

ducted a self-administered sleep learning program in an
attempt to quickly learn enough English to win a BBC
contest. Kohalmir recorded English words matched by
their Hungarian equivalents. Six nights a week for six
weeks, he played the two-hour lesson on a self-repeating
tape during the entire night. His average nightly intake
was thirty-five words or short phrases. Of the 1,284 words
and phrases he recorded, Kohalmir successfully memorized 1,026. He won first prize, which was an all-
expense-paid trip to the United Kingdom. The desire to
travel is credited with providing the motivation to learn.

Sleep learning of a stricter scientific nature has been
conducted in Hungary by Professor Otto Stabel, who has
served as a consultant to the Sleep Learning Association.
Professor Stabel began his work with sleep learning in
the late 1960s. Working with grade school children, he
used nocturnal lessons as an adjunct to regular school-
room teaching. One approach was to teach sleeping students material they would soon be learning in class.

> "I would like to mention that when pupils have
> had to learn at school the material given during sleep
> learning, they have learned it very well and
> quickly."

In another study, Professor Stabel undertook to teach
Morse code signs to a group of fourteen boys and girls
between the ages of twelve and fourteen. The results led
to this report:

> "As learning the Morse code in such a short time,
> at the rate of 40–50 signs per minute, was a con-
> siderable achievement on the part of these children,
> the test proved to us the effectiveness of sleep learn-
> ing and the value of this teaching method."

In France, sleep learning work has been done by Dr. Jacques Genevay, Director of the Laboratory of Applied Psychology in Paris. Dr. Genevay expressed his views on sleep learning in this way:

> "Hypnopaedia not only provides the memory with general working knowledge, but develops that facility of memory which becomes increasingly organized and which makes for increasing suppression of useless effort."

Sleep learning programs have also been successfully conducted in West Germany, Japan, and many other countries throughout the world. In Japan, the sale of sleep learning supplies, including prerecorded tapes, has produced a thriving industry. However, of all the work being done around the world with sleep learning, none can equal in volume or success that conducted in the Soviet Union. The Soviets are the leaders in sleep learning, both experimental and practical. Perhaps one reason for this is the government's involvement in sponsoring sleep learning research programs.

A team of researchers working for the United States Library of Congress concluded that "the Soviet sleep learning research program is extremely well organized and sophisticated. The outstanding feature of the Soviet sleep learning program is the caution and pragmatism exercised by its leaders."

On the subject of American sleep learning programs, the same researchers said: "Apparently, no past or present American research on sleep learning has approached the scope and depth of the current Soviet sleep learning program. Past American efforts have been sporadic, rather poorly organized and inconclusive . . ."

Sleep learning has a long history in the Soviet Union. For over fifty years, Soviet scientists and educators have conducted programs based on the learning of information while asleep. According to a report of the Eighteenth International Congress of Psychology, over five hundred official sleep learning programs have been conducted in the U.S.S.R.

The leading personalities of Soviet sleep learning are Dr. Leonid Andreyevich Bliznitchenko, Director of the Department of Experimental Phonetics at the Potebni Institute of the Ukrainian Academy of Sciences, and Dr. Abram Moiseyevich Svyadoshch, a psychoneurologist who holds a chair in psychiatry at the Karaganda State Medical Institute in Kazakhstan.

Svyadoshch is credited with conducting the first scientific experiments with sleep learning in the Soviet Union. His thesis on the subject, "Speech Perception During Natural Sleep," written in 1937, is considered the foundation stone of Soviet sleep learning. His interest in sleep learning began in 1936 after listening to a patient relate an incident in which she learned the lyrics to a song that was played while she slept. After hearing this, he set about researching whether it was possible for a person to perceive and remember speech that was heard while asleep.

He gathered together one hundred men and women of various ages. All were of normal health. None were told that information would be imparted to them while they were sleeping. During the night, a short story was read twice to each sleeper. Several of them were awakened by the reader's voice, but most remained asleep. The following morning, those who had slept through the readings were asked if they could recall the story. To Professor Svyadoshch's dismay, not one person recalled anything. So, the first experiment conducted by the man who would be called "the father of Soviet sleep learning" ended in complete failure.

Much has been discovered about sleep learning in the

years since this experiment. From our vantage point to-day, we know that Svyadoshch's first attempt failed to include both of the two essential ingredients: constant repetition and motivation to learn. Had even one of these been present, his results would have been more prom-ising.

Disappointed but not discouraged, Svyadoshch ar-ranged for a second sleep learning attempt. This one involved twenty subjects. Each was read a poem twenty times during their sleep. Again, they weren't informed about sleep learning and had absolutely no motivation for learning the poem. The following morning no one recalled it. After the direct recall test failed, he requested each participant to learn and memorize two similar poems. One was the poem used during the sleep learning program.

One person, a twelve-year-old boy, provided a re-markable demonstration of the potential of even such primitive sleep learning methods. He was able to remem-ber the sleep learning poem eight times faster than the other poem. Before entering the program the boy had never heard either poem. Encouraged by this first step toward success, Svyadoshch was joined by other scien-tists, and before long sleep learning experiments were being conducted at several educational and medical fa-cilities.

These two programs, one ending in failure, the other with partial success, gave Soviet researchers the key that opened the door to sleep learning. The key was obvious. Incidental sleep learning is almost unheard of. People have to be aware of the teaching process going on while they sleep. Later sleep learning programs added moti-vation as a second vital factor to successful sleep learning.

Svyadoshch's interests changed over the years, and he shifted his research to the related field of auto-suggestion. Professor Bliznitchenko became the dominant personality and spokesman for Soviet sleep learning. Through his determined efforts, sleep learning received official recognition.

Bliznitchenko first became interested in sleep learning through references to the subject in the works of Soviet science fiction writers. As with Svyadoshch, Bliznitchenko's first attempt at sleep learning ended in failure. It was a simple experiment conducted in 1948 in which he attempted to help a student memorize a text. He used a recorder with a speaker placed near the head of the sleeping person. Undaunted by this setback, Bliznitchenko temporarily set aside actual testing and concentrated his efforts on the study of speech and its relation to sleep learning, especially the intonation of speech and how it is perceived by the listener.

Shortly, however, he returned to the development of practical sleep learning. One of his first programs involved a physician named Galina Vasilyevna Pustogorova, who allowed Bliznitchenko to turn her bedroom into a classroom. For twenty-eight nights, Dr. Pustogorova was taught English, a language of which she had no prior knowledge.

At the conclusion of her sleep learning lessons, Pustogorova was examined by a commission from Kiev State University. To the surprise of the examiners, she did remarkably well. "Pustogorova has a knowledge of the spoken language equivalent to the program of the first course," the commissioners reported. This meant she had learned as much English in twenty-five hours of sleep learning as was normally taught in a one hundred and twenty hour classroom school course.

Sleep learning studies and research programs proceed in the Soviet Union with official sanction, although some portions of the work are shrouded in official secrecy. There have been reports that the Soviet government uses sleep learning to teach foreign languages to its diplomats and intelligence agents. Recent reports indicate that work with school-age children has now expanded to include teaching mathematics, chemistry, and biology, as well as languages.

Whatever the level of success the Soviets have enjoyed working with sleep learning, it's obvious they recognize the value and potential applications available to those who take sleep learning seriously, and have proper motivation.

Sleep Learning Over the Radio

The most unusual method yet tried for sleep learning has been to broadcast lessons over the radio. Sleep learning over the radio has been used in several countries, including the Soviet Union, Czechoslovakia, and the United States. The earliest of these programs took place in September 1965 in the northern Czech city of Pilsen. The radio broadcasts were used to teach English to a group of people selected from the local Lenin Works factory. It was done under the supervision of a linguist, an electrical engineer, a physician, and a lecturer in psychological medicine. The English lessons were broadcast for ten nights. There were three broadcasts of one hour and twenty minutes duration each, starting at 10:15 P.M., 1:15 A.M., and 6:15 A.M. Unfortunately, the results of this program were not made public.

An issue of the journal *Soviet Life* attracted international attention to what may have been the most ambitious sleep learning program undertaken. According to the magazine, sleep learning lessons by radio began in a town not far from Moscow. Working in cooperation with the government agency responsible for radio and television, L.A. Bliznitchenko and a group of scientists from various organizations and institutes directed a program to teach

English to two thousand residents of the town of Dubna.

The sleep learners who participated in this program were a cross-section of the population, ranging in age from sixteen to fifty-eight. They included engineers, scientists, students, actors, and factory and office workers. They all agreed to maintain a firm schedule regarding their sleeping habits, since the lessons were to be broadcast over the local radio station during specific times each night.

Each evening, the participants spent fifteen minutes reading a list of the material to be broadcast that night. This was done at 10:30, when each had already settled into bed. At exactly 10:45 they switched on their bedside radios and listened to a voice read the same material. Following each set of Russian/English words that constituted the lesson, the announcer paused to allow the listeners time to repeat the material aloud. This phase ended at 11:00 P.M., when everyone turned their lights off and went to sleep. Soon after, the lesson was repeated by the announcer in a soft voice until 11:55 P.M.

At 6:30 the following morning, each of the radios came to life again, with the announcer repeating the previous night's lesson several times for twenty-five minutes. All participants awoke at 7:25 A.M. and performed the same routine as the night before, repeating the Russian words and their English translations immediately after the announcer recited each set.

The entire program consisted of thirty-six lessons and lasted nearly two months. No lessons were broadcast on Saturday and Sunday nights. The results of this program varied, based on the individual participant's background and the almost impossible task of thoroughly testing every participant's progress. Many who had previously studied English found the sleep learning lessons revived their dormant knowledge of the language. Those having no previous experience with the language discovered they were able to converse in English within the confines of the words and phrases they learned while asleep.

As a group, those who had no prior knowledge of English were able to learn the first ten lessons completely, while the second ten were learned to a degree of ninety percent. This performance ratio continued to decline, for they mastered only eighty-five percent of the contents of the third set of ten lessons. Total retention for this group was about eighty percent of the material presented over the entire course.

Broadcasting lessons over the radio is a novel approach to sleep learning. The major problem is the difficulty of measuring the results. In May 1973, the *Hospital Tribune* reported on a sleep learning program delivered by radio with potentially far-reaching results. Under the leadership of David Walonick of the University of Minnesota, three educational radio stations participated in a program aimed at helping people kick the smoking habit.

Each night for one week, people in specific areas of the state could tune their radios to the proper station before retiring and, beginning at 1:00 A.M., they would receive the five-hour program. It consisted of an introductory hour of seashore sounds, soft music, and suggestions for relaxing, with the remainder of the time devoted to the anti-smoking message. As a control against which Walonick could check his results, two areas received only the first hour of the broadcast with no anti-smoking message. When the program was announced, the public was told that only one station (each station was located in a different area) would broadcast the full lesson. They weren't told which station.

One week after the program ended, Walonick reported that nearly seventy-two percent of those who heard the entire message claimed they either quit or cut down on their smoking, while twenty-eight percent of those who didn't hear it cut down or quit. He re-canvassed the first group two months later and found twenty-five percent of the group remained successful.

The following year, four radio stations in California took part in another sleep learning program. This time the goal was to reduce the food intake of some listeners while helping others to stop smoking. Throughout the month of September, thousands of Californians in Los Angeles, San Diego, San Jose, and Sacramento set their clock radios to go off at 1:00 A.M. On nights when the weight reduction messages were broadcast, the sleeping participants heard an announcer's voice softly instruct them:

> "Try using small dishes—it makes it look as if there is a lot more on the plate . . . Next time you're tempted by big, scrumptious, gooey desserts, have an apple or an orange instead. Mother Nature makes great desserts, too."

Although scientific methods couldn't be applied to confirm the results, they were impressive. The Los Angeles station received seventy calls each day from "enthusiastic believers" who reported such experiences as, "I woke up this morning and didn't want any breakfast. What did you do to me last night?", or this one from an executive who said:

> "Shortly after the program began I made dinner one night and put it on a small plate. Then I looked at it and said to myself 'Why did I do that?' Later I heard that that was what one of the messages said. I couldn't believe it."

Similar results were reported when this anti-smoking message was broadcast:

"Kissing a smoker is like making love to an ashtray. Former smokers tell us life's easier when both husband and wife don't smoke . . . fewer arguments . . . especially with non-smokers in your life."

Using radio broadcasts for sleep learning is a somewhat exotic approach, but the success experienced by those who have used it over the radio confirms the versatility of sleep learning.

6

Sleep Learning a Foreign Language

How Languages Are Taught

A survey of individuals who have used sleep learning, both in and out of laboratories, reveals the most popular subject is the learning of a foreign language. Language learning is easily adapted to sleep learning since there's no need for visual aids in teaching a language. Repetition is the best way to learn the conversational aspects of any language and, as we've seen, repetition is a key factor in successful sleep learning.

For best results, it is wise to use a language course that is printed in a book or pamphlet. Nighttime lessons should be reviewed during the day. This allows you to use the daily review to reinforce what has been learned during sleep. For maximum results, your nocturnal lessons must follow the structured format of a formal course.

Dr. Brian Dutton of Birbeck College, University of London, offers the following advice for structuring a sleep learning language course:

"... the best method would be to present the roots of words to be used in a given sequence first, with

117

their native equivalents. Next the meaning of the structure could be presented in the native language, and then the two interpreted, possibly with the structure and root meanings also integrated and presented via the native equivalent.''

These suggestions should receive serious consideration from anyone seeking to use sleep learning to acquire a complete knowledge of a foreign language. This kind of language learning can best be accomplished through a combination of sleep learning and regular day sessions. It is not readily adaptable to sleep learning alone. Since sleep learning is a do-it-yourself teaching method, the task of learning is compounded when dealing with complex grammatical construction. Due to the absence of an instructor's supervision, it's advisable for sleep learners to emphasize the conversational use of a language.

Professor Gagne, whose book, *The Condition of Learning*, we referred to earlier, favors learning a foreign language on a conversational level. He recommends that one begin learning a language by first learning common expressions of courtesy and convenience, such as good morning, how are you, good evening, etc. He says that learning simple phrases will increase a person's confidence and will enhance the learning of longer sentences and phrases later, and will ''serve as excellent models from which spontaneous speech can be derived.'' This applies to learning a language by use of sleep learning, and by more traditional methods.

If you're currently attending language classes, sleep learning can enhance your learning capacity and improve your recall. Soviet educators and linguists who have worked with sleep learning agree that combining sleep lessons with regular coursework will significantly accelerate learning.

At a secondary school in Moscow, a group of thirteen

schoolchildren of "average intelligence" were selected to learn German using a combination of day and night lessons. For two months, the students received daily classroom instruction and nightly lessons via sleep learning. Each day and night lesson was forty-five to fifty minutes long. At the conclusion of the course, a group of German language experts examined the children and found "a high technical level of reading of the foreign texts, good pronunciation, fluent translation, the ability to speak quickly, and the correct use of the vocabulary."

During those two months, the group became fluent in 1,000 words, plus 1,900 word combinations of the German language. All this learning took place in a total of sixty-five hours. This compared favorably with Soviet schools that teach German. In a two-year period, a typical foreign language student attends 160 hours of conventional lessons and learns between 900 and 1,000 words.

Professor Bliznitchenko conducted a similar program at another language school. He taught English to four students in their early twenties. Before being introduced to sleep learning, they were attending English classes. One had achieved a rating slightly higher than "satisfactory," but the others were doing poorly. They did not understand any spoken English and were unable to construct a sentence in English without help.

Eighteen nights of sleep learning lessons were administered. Each six to eight minute lesson was played twenty-five times a night. On the nineteenth day, the students were tested on the material used in the sleep learning lessons. One received a rating of "excellent," one a rating of "good," and two were "satisfactory." In addition, the head of the Faculty of Modern Languages said that all four had "acquired the habit of spoken language."

Before moving on, let's look at one final program conducted by Bliznitchenko. Once again, the language taught was English. The course was based on a Russian book titled *Teach Yourself To Speak English*, by S. S. Tolstoi and E. I. Khakina, and combined sleep learning with self-instruction. No instructors participated in the program.

For twenty-two nights, the students listened to tape recordings of English words and phrases. Each evening, two or three presentations of that night's lesson were played before the students went to sleep. Each student followed these presentations visually, using the text of the book and repeating phrases at certain intervals. After they fell asleep, the lessons were repeated twenty-three times per night. By the end of the course, they had learned and remembered an average of 700 English words and expressions, and were able to converse competently in English.

The Ladies Learn German

While it's true the Soviets are the most advanced in the study and use of sleep learning for teaching a new language, they're not alone in the field. A group at England's Sleep Learning Association devised a sleep learning course far different from anything the Soviets had done.

When Mrs. Phyllis Pilgrim and Miss Kirsteen Clark were asked what they thought of the possibility of learning a foreign language while they slept, Mrs. Pilgrim, a twenty-six-year-old schoolteacher, was skeptical of the idea. "I'm not sure whether it's likely to work." Miss Clark, an eighteen-year-old student, was more optimistic, "It seems a good idea," she said.

In spite of any reservations, both women plunged ahead with a program to learn German through sleep learning. Their lessons, which were conducted by the Sleep Learning Association, began on a Monday and ran into trouble the first night. Clark proved to be a restless sleeper who tossed and turned most of the night despite the use of a conditioning tape.

The conditioning tape was intended to help the women relax and induce a sound sleep. This is a method commonly used to calm anxiety that might result from sleeping in a strange environment. For the duration of their sleep training, both women were to sleep in the Association's dormitories, set up especially for sleep learning. Faint, gentle, classical background music was played whenever they entered the dormitories. Both women had previously indicated that they usually fell asleep by midnight, so when they had prepared themselves for bed and had listened to the forty-minute conditioning tape, the automatic timer on the tape player was set to play the lesson tape at midnight.

Ten minutes after the midnight tape began, Mrs. Pilgrim was fast asleep. The restless Miss Clark wrestled with what felt like "an increase in mental activity" and didn't fall asleep until 1:15 A.M. The next night, the conditioning tape was set to start at 11:30. Pilgrim was asleep fifteen minutes later, and Clark in another twenty minutes. The following morning both said they had slept well, although Miss Clark was still apprehensive.

The third night went about the same as the second, with Clark more relaxed than before. This continued the following night. The fifth, sixth, and seventh nights found both women sound asleep fifteen minutes after the conditioning tape began playing. Both reported a restful night's sleep each morning.

During the second week, both Mrs. Pilgrim and Miss Clark were sound asleep before they were presented with a second conditioning tape. They continued to spend restful nights.

On the first night of the third week of their program, the women began their German lessons. The taped lesson contained 185 German words and 219 German phrases. The tape was made in the Association's recording studio by Geoffrey Stocker, who holds teaching degrees in Drama and Speech, and is a native German linguist. The recording gave the German word first, followed by the English translation, followed by the German word again. There was a short pause after each set of words, then the next set was given.

The lesson was played three times on each of the fourteen nights the training lasted. Each night it started at 12:15, turned off at 1:45, began again at 2:45, stopped at 4:00, and the final presentation ran from 6:30 to 7:50. Both women awoke each morning at 8:00. There were a total of twelve repetitions of the lesson each of the fourteen nights.

In the sixth week, a team of examiners, including a representative from London University College, tested Mrs. Pilgrim's knowledge of the German words and phrases taught in the nocturnal lessons. Before the sleep learning course, neither woman knew any German. The test consisted of giving Mrs. Pilgrim the English word or phrase and having her respond with the German translation. The grading system used awarded one point for each completely correct answer and one-half point for an answer that, while perhaps not completely accurate, demonstrated a grasp of the phrase's meaning. Although Mrs. Pilgrim's exam took place at 9:00 P.M. and she was visibly tired, she achieved a recall rate of seventy percent.

Because Miss Clark was taking school exams, her test was delayed for three weeks. Although unplanned, the delay was actually an added benefit, because it served to test her recall of the sleep learning lessons following several weeks without lessons. She was tested in the identical manner as Mrs. Pilgrim. Clark's recall rate was an astonishing ninety-three and one-half percent. Asked what she now thought of learning a language while she slept, she exclaimed, "Sleep learning is a marvelous way to learn."

The significant aspect of this program that distinguishes it from the Soviet approach discussed earlier, is that all learning took place while the women slept. There were no corresponding daytime lessons or review, so that sleep learning was tested as a means of learning in itself rather than a method to increase or improve daytime learning.

A Course in Persian

Before looking at efforts to teach a language through sleep learning in the United States, we'll examine one more language course conducted in Great Britain, under the auspices of the Ealing Technical College, in the dormitories of the Sleep Learning Association.

Four students were selected, two men and two women. The Persian language was used because the students were members of an honors course in applied language studies and Persian bore no resemblance to the languages they were already studying, which were German, Slavic, Italian, and Spanish. Ten lessons were recorded by a native Iranian woman. Each lesson lasted approximately five minutes and consisted of conversational phrases recorded first in English, then in Persian.

Each evening, the students listened to the night's lesson before they went to sleep. The lesson continued to play during the night while they slept. A second set of lessons was used to teach a different series of Persian expressions without the use of sleep learning. The same students served as both the experimental group (learning Persian through sleep learning) and the control group (learning different Persian phrases during the day). When tested on the material from these lessons, the four students had learned an average of over seventy-three percent of the expressions with sleep learning, and slightly less than seventy percent without sleep learning.

That all four were selected from a language honors course and had demonstrated an aptitude for learning through traditional teaching may account for the similarity in performance between day and sleep lessons. Even if the achievement of both forms of learning had been identical, it would still demonstrate that combining sleep learning with regular day lessons can result in learning twice as much in the time normally required for traditional teaching, or learning a comparable amount in half the time. All four students achieved a competent level of fluency in Persian, a good accent, and made few serious errors.

Language Learning in the United States

Although most sleep learning language programs have been conducted across the Atlantic, a few have taken place in America. One of these, conducted at the University of Florida, taught Russian nouns to twenty students while they slept. None of the students had a prior knowledge of Russian.

The sleeping students first heard a conditioning tape, followed by the Russian language lesson, for five consecutive nights. The conditioning message was intended to relax the students and capture their attention while asleep. The tape began:

"This is your Russian teacher; you are asleep and relaxed and you can hear my voice and you will not wake up.... You will remember these words forever."

When the students were tested for their knowledge of the nouns used in the lesson, they had an average recall of thirteen percent, with some as high as thirty percent accurate recall. Thirteen percent success rate is certainly not earthshaking, and although it does prove sleep learning can be used to learn a language, it compares unfavorably with many of the studies previously reviewed. This may be explained if we go back to the laboratory affect discussed earlier. In this program, the sleep learning took place in a laboratory while the sleepers were monitored by EEG. Whether this had an appreciable influence on the results is difficult to say, but it's possible the negative laboratory affect did cause considerable interference.

Two other doctors used a different approach in their sleep learning program. They sought to avoid the potentially distracting effects of both the EEG and the laboratory environment by permitting their sleep learners to remain at home.

Thirty people from the Washington, D.C. area, mostly college students in their early twenties, were selected to participate in this study. Eighteen were men, twelve were women. They were divided into three groups of ten: an experimental group, an interference group, and a control group. While they slept, each group heard a different recording. The experimental group heard twenty-five Chinese words and their English translations. The interference group heard the same Chinese words but with incorrect translations. The control group heard only soothing music.

The lessons were presented for thirty minutes, starting at 2:30 A.M. The participants went to bed at 11:30 P.M. and were instructed to avoid reading, writing, or conversation when they awoke. During the half hour, the lesson was repeated fifteen times. Following is the list of Chinese words and their English translations as they were read to the experimental group.

tien—field	siano—small	rich—day
mu—eye	jia—home	jun—sir
li—strength	sheng—life	dung—east
ta—great	tu—ground	hao—good
ming—bright	ko—may	yen—talk
shao—few	dao—road	sue—snow
lin—grove	fen—knife	wu—five
lo—fall	ali—come	je—this

The program ran for only one night. Although the participants were given a general idea of the purpose of the study, none knew what they would hear while they slept. The recordings were not played to them before they fell asleep.

The following morning, members of the research team visited each sleep learner's home and asked questions concerning their previous night's sleep. Ten subjects said they remembered hearing the tape recorder start. They were disqualified, as this indicated a strong possibility they may have been awakened. When the questioning was completed, each participant was told the researcher would play a tape recording that contained two lists of words.

"There has been recorded on this machine a list of Chinese words and their English equivalents. You are to listen very carefully as they are being played and try to remember the English translation of each of the Chinese words. After the list has been played once you will receive a rest period of several seconds followed by the Chinese words without their English equivalents. You are to try to recall the correct translation of each of these words as they are presented and say them aloud as soon as possible. After this, we will play the original record and continue the same procedure until you have learned the entire list correctly."

The number of times required to replay the list was used as a gauge to test the possibility that the members of the experimental group may have already begun learning the list during their single half hour sleep learning lesson. The Chinese words played during the night were the same for both the experimental and interference groups. The interference group however, heard incorrect English translations.

When the results were compiled, the control group, those who heard only Strauss waltzes, needed an average of almost eight full repetitions of the list before they could give the correct English equivalent to each Chinese word. The experimental group required just five and one-half repetitions before giving the correct answers. This showed that they not only heard what had been presented in that short period during the night, but the correct translations were "saved" in their memories.

But what of the interference group? How were they affected by hearing the wrong translations of the same words? As it turned out, they had to unlearn what they learned during their sleep and re-learn the correct translations of the Chinese words. They required over eleven repetitions to do this, proving that although the information was incorrect, they, too, had learned something during sleep.

Working at Stanford University under grants from the United States Public Health Service and the United States Air Force, Doctors Leslie M. Cooper and J. Hoskovec investigated the use of sleep learning during REM sleep to learn a foreign language. Eleven young men were selected to participate. Their ages ranged from sixteen to twenty-one. All were either high school or college students. Before their selection, they were tested to determine if they were susceptible to hypnosis. In addition, each said he had no knowledge of the Russian language.

The study required that the men sleep in the laboratory for two nights. The first night was to acclimate them to the lab environment. The actual sleep learning was scheduled for the second night, when each was connected to an EEG, eye movement gauges, and an electromyograph. The last was done by applying electrodes to each participant's chin. They slept in a room separated from the researchers by a glass window so they could be visually observed while asleep.

Before being allowed to sleep, each man was hypnotized and given the following post-hypnotic instructions:

"During your sleep we shall speak to you and you will hear and understand what is said to you. You will hear some Russian words and their English translations. You will remember them easily and they will be available to you whenever you wish to repeat them. Of course, you will sleep all the time, not awakening. . . ."

However, the sleep itself was a natural sleep, not hypnotically induced. Hypnosis was used solely to create a suggestion for learning during sleep. While they slept, a list of ten Russian words, each followed by its English translation, was presented. The list was repeated eight times. Since each subject was monitored by EEG, it was possible for Cooper and Hoskovec to administer the lesson during REM sleep only, which they did. Following presentation of the list, the students were awakened. After a five-minute acclimation period, they were tested. Each was given a card listing ten English words and told to select the proper translation for each Russian word as it was pronounced by the researcher. The group achieved an accurate recall of only thirty percent.

The researchers were not impressed by the low scores. While they expressed the belief that the study demonstrated learning probably could take place during REM sleep, they felt it was "possible but not practical."

Although they accomplished only a slight degree of learning, obvious questions arise as to what the result might have been had there been more than eight repetitions of the list, had the list been presented in all stages of sleep, had the students not been wired to three separate monitors, and had they been allowed to sleep through the entire night instead of being awakened immediately after the information was presented to them. Each of these points is important individually, but taken collectively in one study it's questionable whether the results of that study have genuine validity and can be used to challenge the efficacy and practicality of sleep learning.

Repetition of material is essential to learning, and there's no way of knowing if eight repetitions are sufficient for learning the list that was used. Neither do we really know during what phase of sleep material can be presented most effectively. Studies such as this one have been made at most stages and levels of sleep. Overall, the results have been inconclusive in selecting one particular stage of sleep that's best for sleep learning.

Actually, it doesn't appear to matter if any phase of sleep is best. The practical use of sleep learning takes place in the home, not the laboratory. There's no way a sleep learning student can arrange the presentation of a lesson to correspond with a particular sleep stage.

As we know, information processing for memory takes place during sleep. Why then awaken subjects in a sleep learning experiment immediately after the material has been presented? Why not allow time for the information to be processed and test recall after the subjects have awakened naturally?

Another problem with this study is the psychological condition of the students used for sleep learning. The researchers themselves confirmed this when they admitted: "Some of the subjects in this study were anxious, apprehensive, and, in at least one case, rather disturbed by the procedures of sleep learning."

We don't know if these conditions were created by participation in sleep learning or by the inevitable laboratory affect. Whatever the cause, it appears obvious that outside influence had an effect on the results of the study. The major unanswered question with this, as with so many other sleep learning programs conducted in the United States, is: What would the results have been had the European approach been used instead of burdening the students with electronic equipment and the expectation of instant results?

Pamadam
— Drugs.

7

Sleep Learning as Therapy

_____

Sleep Learning as Therapy

Earlier we saw that sleep learning could be used for therapeutic purposes in much the same way as hypnosis. Writing in the Soviet journal *Voprosy Psikhologii*, V. N. Kulikov of the Ivanovo Teaching Institute made the following observation when he was discussing sleep learning as a form of therapy:

> "Therapeutic effects of this method of curing have convincingly shown that the patients in the state of natural sleep absorbed, remembered and retained words suggested by the doctor. Many bad habits can be cured by this method."

In the United States and Canada, sleep learning has been used in numerous therapeutic applications. In some cases, sleep learning techniques have been combined with regular daytime therapy in the treatment of patients diagnosed as chronic psychoneurotics.

Working at the Allan Memorial Institute of Psychiatry in Montreal, Doctors Leonard Levy, D. Ewen Cameron, and Leonard Rubenstein successfully used a program of repetition of negative and positive statements to bring about personality changes in their patients. The statements were recorded on tape and played to the patients usually for sixteen hours a day for twenty days. During most of this time, the patients were maintained in a sleep-like state with tranquilizers.

Many patients receiving this treatment showed dramatic personality improvements, making such comments as feeling like "a different person," "I see things more clearly," and "I get along with people better, I feel more confident."

To accomplish their goal, Dr. Levy and his associates combined what he called the "powerful force" of repetition with the susceptibility to suggestion during sleep. They obtained equally successful results combining sleep learning with regular therapy in the treatment of patients diagnosed as schizophrenic.

Recognizing the influence that susceptibility to suggestion during sleep can have on our behavior, it's not difficult to imagine the potential therapeutic applications of sleep learning. Literature on the subject is full of reports of such therapy. A pediatrician in California reported a seventy percent success rate in curing bed-wetting among children. Several dentists have had success using sleep learning to help patients stop grinding their teeth while they sleep. The directors of a children's camp believe it has helped some of their campers conquer their fear of the water.

A Florida doctor used positive affirmations presented through sleep learning to help a forty-year-old man regain the voice he lost due to psychological reasons at the age of fourteen. Other cases include a minister and a young girl who had both suffered nervous breakdowns. They demonstrated improved strength in dealing with life's problems after sleep learning therapy. The same doctor also claimed successful results with chronic stutterers, insomniacs, and alcoholics.

Individuals who have used sleep learning as self-therapy often report gratifying results, such as breaking a smoking habit. Others claim improved self-confidence with statements such as, "have developed a more positive attitude in dealing with others." A Wisconsin woman says she was able to overcome an acute shyness through sleep learning therapy aimed at improving her self-confidence.

Before John Locke became a judge, he served several years as a public defender. In that position he witnessed firsthand the revolving door effect of the criminal justice system. Month after month, year after year, he would find himself defending the same individuals over and over again. For many, crime had become a normal way of life.

Faced with this depressing, unending cycle, he decided something must be done to help these people get off the treadmill. His response was to develop a program he hoped would help them change their basic attitudes about themselves and their views of society. He solicited financial backing for the program from two local community service organizations and received the support of other Superior and Justice Court judges. The experiment consisted of prerecorded taped messages played to inmates of a county Correctional Center while they were in deep relaxation and sleep.

The inmates, all volunteers for the program, were screened to be certain they recognized that they had personality problems contributing to their anti-social lifestyles. To develop genuine motivation, Locke rewarded each inmate by cutting two days from his sentence for each month he stayed in the program.

The taped messages varied from lessons to improve self-image to those discussing the pitfalls and evils of lawless behavior. Many were recorded by former inmates. Judge Locke called the program "one of the most rewarding experiences of my life."

Unfortunately, accurate records of the results achieved by this sleep learning program were not kept. Locke estimates the success rate at between thirty-five and fifty percent. He based this assessment on the decreased recidivism rate among the participants. In addition, he used sleep learning messages to help several inmates and former inmates overcome addiction to alcohol. Judge Locke described his sleep learning therapy as "aimed at dissolving blocks and inhibitions and encouraging the good within to grow and flower."

Members of both the medical and scientific communities have used sleep learning as a form of therapy. The success they've had may eventually lead to a major breakthrough in therapeutic treatment.

Breaking Bad Habits

The renowned psychologist Lawrence Le Shan was among the first to use sleep learning to break a bad habit. The results he achieved created a totally new dimension in the sleep learning field and identified sleep learning as an effective method to curtail habits such as overeating and smoking.

Dr. Le Shan became interested in the use of sleep learning for habit breaking while he was studying mind conditioning. The connection between the two was natural, since a habit is a conditioned behavior. According to J. P. Chapin's *Dictionary of Psychology*, a habit is "an acquired response," or "an acquired drive . . . which through prolonged practice has become relatively automatic." If a habit is something a person must acquire through the conditioning of practice, it's logical to assume the habit can be broken through reverse conditioning.

Dr. Le Shan theorized that the required conditioning might be achieved by suggestions made to sleeping people with bad habits they wanted to break. The site selected for putting this theory to the test was a summer camp for boys in New York State. The habit chosen as the target for nocturnal suggestion was common among boys, nail biting. Forty habitual nail biters were found among the one hundred and thirty-five youths at the camp. They were divided into three groups. Twenty boys ranging in age from eight to twelve were placed in the experimental group to whom the anti-nail biting sleep suggestions would be made. Eight others were classified as control group A, while control group B was composed of the remaining twelve boys. Dr. Le Shan recorded a message in a normal speaking voice, repeating the following sentence fifty times: "My fingernails taste terribly bitter."

The twenty boys in the experimental group heard the message six times each night while they slept. They were not told about the nighttime message. The recording wasn't turned on until each member of the group had been asleep for at least two and one-half hours. Under the guise of a routine medical examination, each boy was checked regularly. The means of determining if any boy had stopped biting his nails was simple. Since all forty habitually kept their nails bitten to stubs, any absence of biting would be immediately obvious. No attempt was made during the day to influence the boys in any way.

The first sleep learning suggestions began on July 5. During the medical exam on August 7 it was discovered that one member of the group had stopped biting his nails. Thirteen days later, two more boys had stopped. The final suggestions were given during the night of August 28. The following day's examination revealed five additional nail biters had stopped, bringing the total number to eight of the twenty boys in the experimental group. In the meantime, there was no change in the nail biting habit of the members of the two control groups, none of whom heard the sleep learning suggestions.

With the acceptable success rate of forty percent, Dr. Le Shan was being conservative when he concluded that the results indicated a definite therapeutic application of suggestion during sleep. Although the results of this experiment lend exciting support to the possible applications of such habit breaking therapy, it is even more stimulating to consider what the rate of success might have been if the group had been first motivated to break their habit and were made aware of the nightly help they were receiving.

The *Los Angeles Times* published a story titled "Mental Suggestion May Help Fat Reducing Diet." Quoting a university professor and medical doctor that ninety-nine percent of overweight people are that way because they overeat, the story described "an interesting and effective way to solve this problem" that "re-educates and reconditions" the overeater with suggestions made during sleep. The suggestions consisted of telling the sleeper he no longer had an abnormal appetite and now had tremendous willpower to resist food that had previously been irresistible.

Earlier we saw the similarity in susceptibility to suggestion between hypnosis, deep relaxation, and certain stages of sleep. Hypnosis has been used on a wide scale for years to help people break habits when they are committed to do so. Clearly those who have the necessary motivation to break a habit will be able to accomplish this through a self-administered sleep learning conditioning program.

Helping a Stroke Victim

When Mr. M., a director of a British shipping company, suffered a stroke, it caused almost total impairment of his ability to speak. Before the stroke, the fifty-one-year-old, highly educated bachelor was considered an intelligent and articulate man.

The stroke left Mr. M. with a spontaneous vocabulary of only two words, "yes" and "no." These were the only words he could use correctly in forming any type of responsive conversation. He also could not count, supply the name of any object shown him, or comply with a simple command such as pointing to some object. Three years of therapy at the Speech Therapy Department of St. Margaret's Hospital in Epping, England resulted in steady but slow progress. The therapy included taped repetitions of speech. The lessons were tape-recorded so the highly motivated Mr. M. could give himself his daily lesson when it was convenient and he could concentrate without distractions.

Before sleep learning was introduced into his therapy, Mr. M. had a spontaneous vocabulary of ten words and could count to three. He would imitate almost any word spoken to him and, using the same repeating method, could count to ten. After two weeks of sleep learning lessons he was able to correctly pronounce thirteen of the twenty-eight words used in the lessons, for a net gain of nine words.

He was then given a continuous-run tape that contained twenty new words. A tape recorder with an automatic timer which started the tape one and one-half hours after he fell asleep was used. The lesson played for one hour, then again for a second hour just before his normal waking time. After a week of these nocturnal lessons, with no help at all during the day, Mr. M. was responding to ten of these new words.

During the next week, he was given day lessons in combination with the sleep learning sessions. At week's end he had improved by five more words, for a net gain of fifteen words in four weeks. The third portion of Mr.

M.'s treatment consisted of thirty-two words which he learned during combined night and day lessons. After two weeks, he gained an additional twenty-five words. The therapist summarized Mr. M.'s treatment program with the following comment:

> "... the results do seem to show that spontaneous recall was increased when the patient received day and night help. Recall of words given during sleep alone appeared to be similar in number to those gained from daytime alone."

Teaching Brain Damaged Children

Dr. Thayne A. Hedges conducted a sleep learning program to help teach speech to children with brain damage. Dr. Hedges' pupils suffered from "delayed speech," a term used to describe those who have difficulty acquiring speech. The children selected for the program were considered "severely delayed" due to either mental deficiency or aphasia. Aphasia is a condition in which the brain doesn't maintain a normal rate of development due to lesions in its upper regions, resulting in a loss of speech or understanding of language. These were children so badly afflicted that progress was measured by how long it took them to learn new sounds or by increases in their verbal "babblings."

Two of the three children involved in this program failed to demonstrate results significant enough to be attributed to the sleep learning lessons they received. The third child is of singular interest, because there is clear evidence that sleep learning contributed to his improvement. This six-and-one-half-year-old boy, whom we'll call Frank, was diagnosed as "... either childhood aphasia or mental retardation; probably both. Retarded speech; about two to two and one-half year level with articulation much more retarded."

To determine the effect of the nocturnal lessons on Frank's progress, he was given two separate series of lessons, one with sleep learning, the other without. Each series was based on teaching him to properly pronounce a consonant. Success would be measured by his ability to pronounce it in isolation and when used in three different locations in words: at the start of a word, in the middle of a word, and at the close of a word.

The first lessons in Frank's program, without the help of sleep learning, were used to teach him to pronounce "f." The sleep learning aided lessons were used to teach him "th." The first lessons ran for one-half hour every other day, for a total of three lessons each week. Progress was extremely slow. By the end of the twenty-fifth lesson, Frank's instructor reported that he was able to consistently use "f" in conjunction with vowels but had only inconsistent usage when used as part of words.

The second set of lessons began with daytime sessions only, each identical to the first series in length and timing. At the end of the eleventh lesson, Frank's instructor considered his progress to be only "fair." At this point, sleep learning lessons were introduced. They were recorded by the same instructor who worked with the child during the day. Since this series of lessons was concerned with the use of "th," this was the basis of the recorded lessons. Following is the lesson used for the sleep training, just as it was recorded and played for the boy.

Stick out your tongue, Frank.
Not quite so far—just a little bit.
That's it. Now blow some air.
thah (repeated three times)
tha (repeated three times)

thih (repeated three times)
thee (repeated three times)

Now let's make some words, Frank. Stick
out your tongue. Not so far. Just a
little bit. That's it. Blow some air.
think (repeated six times)
thank you (repeated seven times)

Now let's blow at the other end of the
word, Frank.
with (repeated three times)
teeth (repeated three times)
tooth (repeated three times)
thank you Frank ("th" accented)
thank you ("th" accented)

Two days after the first sleep learning lesson, Frank
attended his twelfth regular half hour lesson. The instructor reported that his lesson produced a good consistent use of "th" when used in isolation and showed that progress had been made in using it with vowels.

Frank completed six nights of sleep learning lessons in seven days. One night was lost because a storm disrupted electric service. He also missed his next regular session with his instructor. When he returned for his thirteenth daytime lesson, all nocturnal sessions had been completed. Use of "th" in isolation had improved, as well as when used with vowels. In addition, there was improvement when using words that started or ended with "th." By the twentieth lesson, he was described by his instructor as "consistently good" when using "th" at the beginning and at the close of words, but still had difficulty with words in which "th" appeared in the center.

A review of the recorded sleep learning lessons showed that no words with "th" in the center were used. This would account for his failure when using "th" in this way. Comparing the results of the two series of lessons, we find that without the help of sleep learning, Frank required twenty-five lessons to gain only inconsistent use of "f" in all three positions. When sleep learning was used, Frank needed only twenty lessons to acquire consistent use of "th" at the beginning and end of words. The area in which he was inconsistent, when used in the center of a word, wasn't included in the sleep learning lessons.

An interesting incident occurred on the mornings following the last two sleep learning lessons. When Frank's mother entered his room to turn off the recorder, she found him, still "drowsy and half asleep," lying in his bed talking back to the recorded lesson. He was accurately following the instructor's directions.

Dr. Hedges concluded: "Besides the difference in the overall time element required for each consonant, the 'th' progress immediately improved after the introduction of the auditory stimuli during sleep."

The recorded lessons used for the two other children involved in the program were suspect, and reveal a substantial difference in the approaches used. Looking back on the lessons, Dr. Hedges felt that in one case they contained too many words and had too much variety. The second child's sleep learning lessons had wide-ranging time intervals between repetitions, and changes of voice pitch were used by the instructor who recorded the lessons. Here also, Hedges felt fewer words should have been introduced. He also speculated that better results might have been obtained had Frank received more sleep learning lessons.

Nevertheless, this extremely limited attempt to use sleep learning to improve the progress of children with brain damage did demonstrate its potential if the technique is used correctly. Although we might say that sleep learning did not have a dramatic effect on Frank's progress, obviously its contribution to improved speech was small. That contribution is enhanced by the fact that the lessons did not interfere with regular daytime treatment, but augmented it during a time that would otherwise have been lost as far as therapy was concerned.

Victor was a seventeen-year-old with a brain injury that caused him to have serious reading problems and poor visual and auditory memory. The traditional educational therapy used in such cases is based on reinforcement training to recognize sounds and to synthesize these sounds.

Working at the Northside Center for Child Development in New York City, Cecelia Pollack decided to add sleep learning as part of Victor's treatment. She hoped it would provide the amount of repetitions that seemed to be required to help the young man blend sounds to form words. At the time, Victor was functioning at an extremely low level despite his participation in courses for slow learners.

When he was tested by a remedial reading therapist three years earlier, he was classified as "a total non-reader with a short attention span." Just before starting his sleep learning lessons, his vocabulary consisted of less than fifty words. Any gains he made were always offset by an abnormal amount of forgetting. In spite of this, Victor's motivation and desire to read remained high.

Victor's new treatment program was based on two lists of words; an experimental list and a control list. Each contained twenty-three letter-words considered to be of equal difficulty in learning. On the first day, he was taught the words on the control list once and tested for results. Four days later, he was taught and tested the same words. The same procedure was done twice more. Records were kept of his progress at each session.

When work on the control list was completed, he went through the identical procedure with the words on the experimental list, with one exception. Each night during the period this list was taught, Victor was treated to sleep learning as a means of reinforcing the lessons. The experimental list was recorded on a tape preceded by the following statement:

"Victor, this is your reading teacher, Mrs. Pollack, talking to you. I know you want to learn to read as quickly as possible. It will help you to read if you will learn the list of words I am about to read to you.

You are completely relaxed, but part of your mind is concentrating on what I am saying. Listen carefully, Victor. You will remember and keep on remembering the words I say to you even after you have awakened in the morning after a night's refreshing sleep."

One hour after Victor fell asleep and one hour before his scheduled awakening, the tape recorder played for one-half hour. The testing was consistent through every session; Victor was given thirty seconds to synthesize the sounds necessary to properly say each word. Within that time period was permitted three attempts at each word. The results were truly astounding, and provoked Mrs. Pollack to remark: "On the basis of the results of this study therefore, it is possible to conclude that sleep learning can hasten the process of learning to synthesize sounds into words."

Let's review the results. At the first session with the control list, Victor learned to pronounce eight words on the first attempt, one word on the second try, and one word on the third, leaving ten words classified as "unknown." This was also his performance at the first session with the experimental list.

By the fourth session with the control list, he was able to say thirteen words on the first try, two on the second, and none on the third try. Five words were left "unknown." At the fourth session with the experimental list, Victor successfully pronounced eighteen words on his first attempt and two words on his second, leaving none for the third or the "unknown" classification. Victor's progress prompted his therapist to call for further studies using sleep learning on patients like Victor.

Cerebral Training

Perhaps the most fascinating therapeutic application yet made of sleep learning is Cerebral Training. Created by Dr. Ernst Schmidhofer, a clinical neurophysiologist, Cerebral Training combines daytime training classes with sleep suggestion. Although now fifty years old, Cerebral Training is still considered a pioneering concept for the treatment of individuals suffering from psychiatric or emotional disorders.

Dr. Robert M. Friedenberg of the University of Maryland's Psychiatric Institute said of Cerebral Training: "If it were possible for any one method to offer hope and meaning to all groups and persons of society, then Cerebral Training would come close."

Dr. Schmidhofer began developing his program in 1944. At the time, he was in charge of two "violent wards" at the Aiea Heights Naval Hospital, Pearl Harbor. Most of his patients were Marines who were brought in from various South Pacific battle scenes. He described the condition of these men as running the gamut of classic psychiatric symptoms.

Cerebral Training grew out of Dr. Schmidhofer's efforts to develop a mental health treatment program for these patients who were otherwise receiving only minimal attention, due in part to staff shortages. What evolved was a program with three primary objectives: relieve people of their symptoms, teach them how to solve their own problems and teach them to think straight. In many respects, Cerebral Training is a self-help treatment system requiring that the patients, or as Schmidhofer calls, them, "trainees," have the desire to overcome their problems.

"My approach," he says, "is not that of a physician; instead it is of an 'instructor'. We adopt the view that very many disorders and derangements have been learned, which in turn can be unlearned."

During the day, the trainees took part in various activities, including listening to prerecorded recitations and reading specially designed booklets while they engaged in work therapy. Each night while they slept, they were presented with recorded affirmative statements such as, "I can rid myself of any symptoms. I am not overly dependent on medicines or doctors."

These messages began shortly before the trainees went to sleep and continued throughout the night until about thirty minutes after they awakened. This intensive program of nightly recordings and daytime readings obtained extraordinary results. At the naval hospital, it produced peaceful nights for Marines who had previously been unable to sleep through a single night. There was a dramatic improvement in their emotional and mental condition, which permitted many to sleep less fitfully and without the persistent terror dreams that had haunted them.

After only two weeks in the program, several trainees reported being able to nap during the day and sleep throughout the night for the first time in a long time. Dr. Schmidhofer has since put his program into place at institutions throughout the country, with results equal to or better than those at the naval hospital in Pearl Harbor.

8

Sleep Learning and You

Becoming a Sleep Learner

At the outset we stated that using sleep learning successfully "requires a thorough understanding of how and why it works." Although it may be possible for some people to buy the necessary equipment, record a few lessons, and begin learning while they sleep, we have seen in the preceding chapters that your chances of successful sleep learning are greatly enhanced by careful preparation for the experience.

Part of that preparation is the belief in your own ability to process information heard during sleep. Unlike brainwashing, sleep learning cannot be forced on you. You must have the motivation to learn and believe in what you're doing. This belief should be based on what you have already learned about the components of sleep learning.

We know that sleep learning makes use of our subconscious as the conduit of information. We also know that information most easily enters our subconscious when we are not fully conscious. The resistance of our conscious mind is reduced as we slip away from consciousness and produce a condition in which the subconscious mind readily accepts ideas suggested to it. Sleep offers this condition, and sleep learning gives us the opportunity to exploit it.

Your personal success will depend on these four factors:

1. your attitude toward this method of learning;
2. the material you wish to learn;
3. the strength of your motivation; and
4. how well you prepare your lessons.

Geoffrey Stocker, founder of the Sleep Learning Association, says the sleep learner must play two roles: a scientist and an artist. The scientist in us must conduct our own quasi-experiments to find our individual approach to sleep learning. The artist must then create the sleep learning program that will produce the best results. All this may sound complex, but it's really a matter of simple deduction, as you'll see in this and the following chapter.

Let's recap what we have learned and see how that information will help you become a successful sleep learner.

Through the experiences of people such as Bonnie Cashin and Bernard Baruch, we have witnessed the creative and problem-solving powers of our subconscious. We know that the best time for bypassing the roadblock function of the conscious mind and reaching down into our center of creativity is during sleep. The psychological resistance presented by the conscious mind forces us to be active participants in the learning process and, therefore, active learners. When we employ sleep to overcome that resistance, we allow ourselves to become passive learners, but learners just the same. Aldous Huxley said that the effectiveness of suggestions made below our threshold of awareness is increased as the level of resistance decreases.

In one of the experiments we reviewed, we saw the result of sending visual pictures directly to the subconscious without permitting the conscious mind to play its role. Similar studies prove that data entering our subconscious without our active participation is quickly transformed into information easily used by our conscious mind. In one case, the conscious mind used this information that entered through the subconscious to create "subconscious art."

In that case, the researcher succeeded in reaching the subconscious while awake. Countless others have verified our ability to do so while we're asleep. Dr. Anthony Ruffino and Professor A. M. Svyadoshch showed us how direct learning takes place during sleep.

Programs done at prestigious institutions prove that sleeping individuals can not only hear while they sleep, but what they hear can influence their dreams and cause them to react physically to a variety of stimuli while asleep. The snoring mathematics professor showed that a person can make use of the intellectual process necessary to correct erroneous information, even while asleep. It's evident that we can hear while we sleep, that we can react to what we hear, and that sleep is an ideal time for information to reach into our subconscious memory. But in order for that information to be useful, we must be able to recall it when needed.

When another researcher taught his sleeping subjects English/Russian translations, he used a re-learning test to evaluate their ability to retain what they heard. He then compared that ability successfully with the same subjects' ability to learn a different set of translations while they were awake. These findings were confirmed by the results achieved at Duke University by yet another researcher, who said the evidence he found supported the belief that information presented during sleep is retained and can be used later when tested.

Professor L. A. Bliznitchenko was emphatic on this subject: "Information introduced into the human memory by hypnopaedic (sleep learning) means is retained. And it can be effectively reproduced by the subject just as information received in the waking state."

In our discussion of the proactive and retroactive inhibitions to learning and memory, we saw how sleep aids our ability to memorize information. Scientific studies confirm that learning followed immediately by sleep is "perfectly retained." The famous Dallenbach study at Cornell proved that subjects who slept right after learning retained over twice as much information as they did if they remained awake following their learning. In his book *How to Improve Your Memory*, Professor James D. Weinland concluded that ". . . in learning something on which you are to be tested the next day, it would be best to learn it in the evening just before bedtime and review it the next day shortly before the test."

Since sleep is an invaluable tool in processing learning and memory, it is obvious that information presented to our sleeping mind will enter this process without being hindered by the usual outside interference factors.

Preparing Yourself for Sleep Learning

Now that we understand how and why sleep learning works, we can discuss how you prepare yourself for sleep learning. We have seen from the sleep learning studies discussed earlier, both the successful and the unsuccessful, that proper preparation is essential for favorable results.

Before engaging in sleep learning, examine your own sleeping habits. If you have a tendency to stay awake late into the night with only short periods of sleep, or are a restless sleeper, you should practice the relaxation techniques discussed later in this chapter. It is important that you become a restful sleeper so your sleep learning lessons will not awaken you.

Many sleep learners report that using sleep learning has actually improved the quality of their sleep. In fact, Professor Svyadoshch claims that "fatigue from the assimilation of information during natural sleep appears to be less than from its assimilation during the waking state." In other words, sleep learning is less tiring than other forms of learning.

Once you have made the decision to learn while you sleep, it is important that you examine your attitude toward sleep learning and the goals you hope to accomplish through this teaching method. Now is the time to ask yourself these questions:

1. Do I understand how sleep learning works?
2. Has this understanding convinced me of my own ability to learn while I sleep?
3. What are my reasons for wanting to use sleep learning?

Because successful sleep learning relies on several psychological factors, it is vital that you, the prospective sleep learning student, be properly prepared for this experience. To help you determine your readiness, consider these questions one at a time.

Although sleep learning is a complex psychological phenomenon that makes use of human capacities and functions about which we have limited knowledge, explaining how it works in layman's terms is easy.

Based on what we learned from earlier chapters, we have gained the following knowledge of sleep learning:

- Sleep learning is a method of teaching while the pupil is in deep relaxation or a state of sleep.

- While in either of these states, an individual's conscious mind is in a phase of declined use.

- Since the conscious mind acts as a discriminating roadblock against information reaching the subconscious, sleep learning is a technique of introducing material directly to the human subconscious.

- The subconscious absorbs information the way a dry sponge absorbs water.

- The subconscious then stores that information in a vast warehouse of knowledge.

- Sleep learning is learning by suggestion, although it is not necessary to be highly suggestible to be a successful sleep learner.

The information presented in this volume should have provided you, the prospective sleep learner, with enough confidence to answer the first question, "Do I understand how sleep learning works?", with a definite "Yes."

The second question, "Has this understanding convinced me of my own ability to learn while I sleep?", concerns whether the case for sleep learning has been sufficiently persuasive to convince you that you will be able to learn while you sleep. In the preceding chapters we reviewed several controlled experiments. Some of these had varying degrees of success, while others failed. Without becoming immersed in scientific jargon, we have attempted to identify the ingredients that comprise the success or failure of these experiments.

Those factors that contributed most substantially to successful sleep learning are summarized as follows:

1. The sleep learning student was properly motivated;

2. a limited amount of material was presented in each lesson;

3. the lessons were recorded so that they were repeated many times over; and

4. each lesson was usually preceded by a statement designed to strengthen the sleep learner's motivation to learn and remember the information in the lesson.

The sleep learning failures have been characterized by both a laboratory environment and the use of electronic equipment wired to the participants. The emphasis some researchers have placed on measuring the various stages of sleep has retarded the positive effects of learning while asleep. Hopefully, the evidence presented here offers the conclusive proof required to convince you that sleep learning is an effective way to learn. There's no known reason it shouldn't work for the overwhelming majority of people who can be helped by sleep learning.

Do You Really Want to Learn?

One essential element in learning successfully is the motivation of the individual. This motivation is at the heart of the answer to the third question, "What are my reasons for wanting to use sleep learning?" Your answer must be that the reason is one that results in a strong desire on your part to learn. Motivation plays an even greater role in sleep learning than it does in any other method of learning. In the sleep learning programs and studies we have reviewed, it was obvious that the lack of motivation to learn the material being presented was a key factor in those attempts that failed; and, conversely, the presence of strong motivation was a crucial ingredient when sleep learning was achieved.

The absence of motivation played a clear part in the inability of sleep learning volunteers to learn and memorize lists of nonsense syllables in many of the early sleep learning programs. When the importance of motivation to successful sleep learning became obvious, researchers took steps to insure their pupils had the impetus to learn the nocturnal lessons. When one researcher taught Russian vocabulary to his sleeping volunteers, he paid a bonus to those who were able to recall what had been taught while they slept. In other cases, students were selected based on their desire to learn the material being taught.

Professor L. A. Bliznitchenko was emphatic on the importance of motivation to successful sleep learning when he said: "In practice, healthy persons of any age can make successful use of this method (sleep learning) for the memorization of appropriate information. The student simply needs to prepare himself for such work, and to show a desire for the assimilation of information."

While it is true that some individuals have successfully learned material during sleep when they have not been motivated, the importance of motivation to any type of learning cannot be overemphasized. You will recall that Robert Gagne identified motivation as an essential ingredient of learning. Although the physical act of learning while you sleep is a simple one, preparing yourself psychologically and preparing your lessons requires your commitment of time and effort. To engage in these preparations without being truly motivated to learn will be foolhardy. Before you decide to launch a sleep learning program, you must examine your reasons for wanting to do so. You are the only one who can answer the question: Do you really want to learn?

Each potential sleep learning student must examine his or her reasons for using sleep learning. Sleep learning is not something that one engages in for fun. It is a serious process of learning that can be extremely helpful to the student with a genuine desire to acquire knowledge. If you honestly possess the desire to learn and believe that sleep learning is a method to aid you in learning, then you have properly prepared yourself for the experience of learning while asleep. Remember, this desire cannot be faked. If this basic factor is absent, it will have a negative affect on your ability to learn while sleeping.

If you understand how sleep learning works, recognize your ability to learn while asleep, and have a true desire to learn while asleep, you have established the psychological set that is imperative to successful sleep learning.

Selecting What You Want to Learn

What can be learned through sleep learning? Professor Bliznitchenko is convinced that by introducing and consolidating information in the human memory during sleep, we can greatly enhance our ability to learn in "many fields of knowledge and social activity." As examples, he cites foreign languages, mathematics, physics, telegraphy, geography, economics, and psychotherapy.

Virtually anything that can be learned through verbal communication can be learned through sleep learning. Students can use sleep learning to memorize important dates and events for history courses, formulas for chemistry classes, tables for mathematics, or rules for composition courses. Business professionals can use it to remember financial statistics, productivity standards, or foreign languages so important in today's international commerce.

Public speakers can learn and remember vast amounts of information, as well as anecdotes and humorous stories to help get them through a speech. Actors and actresses can learn their lines while asleep. Diplomats and ordinary travelers no longer need to grapple with the intricacies of a foreign language. By selecting from the many prerecorded language courses available to the public, almost anyone can learn a foreign language. Whatever you desire to learn, you will be able to learn it through sleep learning.

When selecting a subject, choose one you genuinely want to learn. Remember that motivation plays a key role in your success. Although incidental sleep learning may help you learn a subject, success can be elusive if you lack a real desire to learn the subject you have chosen.

After choosing your subject, you must decide whether to record your own lessons or use professionally prepared tape recordings. Companies that offer recorded tapes for sleep learning have an extremely wide selection from which to choose. Examples of tapes commercially available include those for use in helping to alter eating habits for weight reduction or weight gain, for strengthening willpower, for improving concentration and self-control, and for a wide variety of other self-confidence building purposes.

When sleep learning a language, an approach that falls between using a professional tape and recording your own lessons is to record the material directly off a record. Most large libraries have a selection of language course records. These usually come with a small booklet containing a printed version of the lessons included on the record. The lessons used on these records are usually prepared by companies or schools who offer professional language courses, and frequently the recordings are made by individuals native to the language being taught. Because of this, recording your lessons from these records may prove to be the best approach to learning a language while you sleep.

If your sleep learning goal is a form of self-improvement, you still have the option of purchasing professional recordings or making your own. Whatever you decide to learn through sleep learning, you will find it beneficial to begin with something simple. This will allow time to acclimate yourself to the experience of learning during sleep, and help you develop the best techniques for your personal success.

Relaxation Methods

A vital factor for successful sleep learning is the complete relaxation of the student, both physically and emotionally. Learning can be faster and easier if we are first able to relax and reduce our levels of emotional and physical stress. Although sleep time is usually accompanied by reduced stress, it is possible for the stress of daily activities and experiences to interrupt peaceful sleep. Sometimes new sleep learners may find that the experience of learning something while they sleep is stressful in itself. Whether or not this happens to you, it is important for your success to practice some technique that reduces stress and promotes a state of relaxation.

There are numerous relaxation or stress reduction techniques. These three I feel are most appropriate for sleep learners to incorporate as part of their preparation for learning during deep relaxation and sleep. You are free to choose from among these three, or any others. What is important is that you select one that works best for you.

A word of caution before describing these relaxation methods. When practicing any physical unstressing technique, it is important that you remember that the muscles of your body will likely reach a depth of relaxation that will require several minutes to return to their normal level of tension. You should avoid attempting to rise suddenly from your relaxed position until your body has recovered its normal muscle tone. Once you have selected a relaxation technique and practiced it, you should prepare the timing device that will operate the sleep learning lesson before begin your relaxation program. Once relaxed, you do not want to get up to set the tape recorder and timer, or you will defeat the purpose of relaxing.

Progressive Relaxation

The first technique is called Progressive Relaxation. Originally developed at Harvard in the early part of this century by Edmond Jacobson, Progressive Relaxation is based on the theory that high levels of anxiety and low levels of muscular tension are incompatible with each other. In other words, anxiety can be reduced by reducing muscular tension in the body. In 1938, Jacobson identified fifteen muscle groups he said were related to tension and relaxation of the body. He then detailed a systematic procedure for training an individual in the deep relaxation of these muscles through alternately contracting and relaxing them. Jacobson's procedure required a professional practitioner's presence during fifty-six sessions stretching over several months.

In the intervening years, a modified version of Jacobson's Progressive Relaxation was developed by Dr. Joseph Wolpe. It required only six clinical sessions, with the balance of the relaxation training done at home. Since our primary goal is sleep learning, we will adapt that modified approach to self-administered home use.

But first, an explanation of how Progressive Relaxation works. The reason for contracting or tensing the muscles before relaxing them is that following the stress caused by tensing, relaxing them will lower their tension level far below the normal level. By raising the electrical activity of the muscles well above the normal level and then suddenly releasing the tension, the electrical activity plummets to an extremely low level, much like the cars on a roller coaster climb slowly to the first, and usually highest, peak and then plunge steeply after reaching the top.

The following Progressive Relaxation procedure was developed for right-handed persons. Those who are left-handed should reverse the right/left sequence of the hands, arms, legs, and feet.

Assuming that you are already in bed, lie back and close your eyes. Keep your eyes closed during the entire procedure. Clear your mind of all thoughts other than the goal of relaxing. Think about your body. Scan it mentally for any areas of tension you can feel and try to relax those areas. Your breathing should be calm and relaxed.

Take a deep breath and hold it for a moment. Concentrate on the muscles in your chest and see if you can feel their pressure. Slowly allow the air out and let your entire body relax. Your breathing should return to a calm rhythm. Repeat this deep breathing process and let your body sink into the bed. As you go through the following steps, your mind should concentrate on each region of your body that you are tensing and relaxing. All inhaling and exhaling should be done slowly.

Step 1   Right hand and forearm—Make a tight fist and inhale for seven seconds. You will feel the tension in your hand, over your knuckles, and in your lower arm. Exhale and permit the hand to become very relaxed for thirty to forty seconds.

Step 2   Upper right arm—While keeping the muscles in your hand and forearm relaxed, push your elbow down against the bed by tightening your bicep, and inhale, holding that position for several seconds. Exhale and allow the muscles in your upper arm to become loose and limp.

Step 3   Left hand and forearm—Follow the same procedure as Step One.

Step 4   Upper left arm—Follow the same procedure as Step Two.

Step 5   Forehead—As you inhale, slowly raise your eyebrows as high as possible. Hold this pose for several seconds as you feel the muscles in your forehead and scalp tense, then exhale and permit those muscles to become very relaxed.

Step 6   Upper cheeks, nose, and eyes— Squint your eyes as tight as possible and wrinkle your nose as you inhale. A few seconds of this and you exhale and allow the muscles around your eyes and upper face to relax.

Step 7   Lower cheeks and jaws—As you inhale, pull the corners of your mouth back in a tight grimace and clench your teeth together, not too tightly. You'll feel the tension all through the lower part of your face and jaw. After a few seconds, exhale and let your jaw and mouth relax.

Step 8   Neck and throat—Contract the muscles in your throat as you simultaneously pull your chin down toward your chest and prevent it from touching your chest. After a few seconds, exhale and allow your neck to become very relaxed.

Step 9   Chest, shoulders, and upper back—As you take a deep breath, pull your shoulder blades together as if you were trying to make them touch each other. Exhale slowly and permit your shoulder muscles to relax.

Step 10   Abdominal region—Inhale and tighten your stomach muscles hard, then exhale and relax. You will begin to feel your entire body slipping into a deep relaxation.

Step 11   Right thigh—Tense the muscles in your thigh as hard as you can and inhale. Hold that for a few seconds, then gradually release the breath and the muscles.

Step 12   Right calf—Inhale as you tense the calf muscle and pull your toes toward you for a moment, then relax slowly.

Step 13   Right foot—Increase the tension in your foot by pointing your toes away from you as you inhale. Exhale and allow your foot to become very relaxed.

Step 14   Left thigh—Follow the same procedure as Step Eleven.

Step 15   Left calf—Follow the same procedure as Step Twelve.

Step 16   Left foot—Follow the same procedure as Step Thirteen.

When all the steps have been completed, repeat the entire procedure, then lie quietly and enjoy the sensation of relaxation. One sign that your muscles are deeply relaxed is a feeling of warmth or heaviness in them. You're now ready to begin your sleep learning lesson.

Autogenic Training

While Progressive Relaxation requires your active physical participation, Autogenic Training is a passive relaxation technique. Developed in Germany in 1910 by Dr. Johannes Schultz, Autogenic Training is based on a set of exercises that combine autosuggestion and relaxation. Instead of the tensing and relaxing of muscles practiced in Progressive Relaxation, Autogenic Training attempts similar results—heaviness and warmth of the limbs—through the repetition of key phrases. These can be repeated either orally or mentally.

Whether you are seated or lying down, make yourself as comfortable as possible. The surrounding environment must be peaceful and quiet. Begin repeating the following phrases to yourself, either aloud or mentally, in a slow, soothing manner.

"I feel quite quiet. . . . I am beginning to feel quite relaxed. . . . My feet feel heavy and relaxed. . . . My ankles, my knees, and my hips feel heavy, relaxed, and comfortable. . . . My solar plexus, and the whole central portion of my body, feel relaxed and quiet. . . . My hands, my arms, and my shoulders feel heavy, relaxed and comfortable. . . . My neck, my jaw, and my forehead feel relaxed. . . . They feel comfortable and smooth. . . . My whole body feels quiet, heavy, comfortable and relaxed. . . .

"I feel quite relaxed. . . . My arms and hands are heavy and warm. . . . I feel quite quiet. . . . My whole body is relaxed and my hands are warm, relaxed and warm. . . . My hands are warm. . . . Warmth is flowing into my hands, they are warm . . . warm."

This technique may take some practice before you achieve success, but the time spent in preparation will be worth the results. You will find it helpful to concentrate on each part of your body as it's mentioned during the exercise.

Relaxation Response

Another passive relaxation technique, developed by Dr. Herbert Benson at Harvard's Thorndike Laboratory, is the Relaxation Response. Based in part on Eastern meditation practices, the Relaxation Response offers a simple yet effective formula for achieving relaxation.

As with any relaxation method, you will require a quiet environment in which to practice. You will have to concentrate your attention on a single object, concept, or symbol; a simple one to use is the word "one." A third required ingredient for success is a passive attitude in which you can put all other thoughts out of your mind. No distractions. In Dr. Benson's own words, "A passive attitude appears to be the most essential factor in eliciting the Relaxation Response." Finally, you should be in a comfortable position. Dr. Benson recommends that you not lie down because the Relaxation Response elements will induce sleep. Of course, for our purposes, lying down is exactly what we should be doing.

Once you have accomplished this condition, you are ready to begin the Relaxation Response.

> Lie quietly and close your eyes. Relax your muscles, beginning at your feet and progressing up to your face. Allow them to remain relaxed. Breathe through your nose as you become fully aware of your breathing. As you breathe out, say the word "one" silently to yourself.
> Breathe in . . . breathe out "one."
> Breathe in . . . breathe out "one."
> Breathe in . . . breathe out "one."

Repeat this for ten to twenty minutes. You may open your eyes to check the time, but refrain from setting an alarm clock or other device that will disturb the setting.

Achieving a state of relaxation that will help eliminate the tension and stresses resulting from our daily routines will contribute toward successful sleep learning. All the techniques mentioned here will help you achieve this state.

9

How to Learn
While You Sleep

Selecting the Right Equipment

Early sleep learning programs were burdened by the cumbersome recording devices that used hard discs similar to commercial records. The invention of recording tape simplified sleep learning, making it possible for individuals to practice it on their own. With portable audio cassette recorders/players, sleep learning is not only available to virtually everyone, but has made acquiring the necessary apparatus the simplest part of sleep learning. The cassette recorder/player has also made it possible for sleep learners to record and play their own lessons on the same machine.

You will need only four items to begin your sleep learning lessons. These are: (1) a cassette tape player: (2) a continuous loop cassette tape that repeats your lessons over and over; (3) a speaker or earpiece that enables you to hear the lessons while you sleep; and (4) a timing control device that plays your lessons at the required times.

Cassette Tape Player

Although it is possible to use a record player for sleep learning, it is more practical to use a tape cassette machine. Not only is it easier to handle, but it allows you to record and erase lessons on the same machine and is relatively inexpensive. A glance through most Sunday newspapers will likely produce several advertisements for cassette recorder/players on sale for as little as $30. Such inexpensive units are suitable for sleep learning, provided their sound reproduction is of sufficient quality to minimize surface noises.

When shopping for your recorder/player, look for three features the machine must have: It must operate by electricity, it must have an external speaker jack, and it must be equipped with a full-range volume control. A machine that operates solely by battery is inappropriate for sleep learning, since it will not permit a preset timing of lessons. The external speaker jack should be the type that automatically shuts off the tape player's internal speaker when the jack is plugged in. This will allow better control over the volume of your lessons and help avoid disturbing the sleep of others nearby. A quality player of any price will have a volume control with a full range of settings rather than merely low and loud. This feature is important, because it provides the option of choosing the level of sound that you can hear while asleep, but will not awaken you.

Endless Loop Tape

Although some cassette players now include an automatic reverse feature for continuous play, the least complex method for the uninterrupted playing of your lessons is an endless loop cassette. This differs from an ordinary cassette because it contains one spindle instead of two. As the name implies, the tape forms one loop that travels from the spindle, through the cassette, and back to the spindle again without stopping. It repeats the same message over and over again until the machine is shut off. These "endless" tapes are available in a wide assortment of running times, from three minutes to as long as one hour. Based on what we have learned from previous sleep learning programs, I recommend that you use a tape that has a message length of between twelve and fifteen minutes. This means your lesson will be repeated about four times each hour the machine is on. Depending on the complexity of the material, you may choose to use a shorter tape.

Pillow Speaker

The next item on our shopping list is an external speaker. Several different types of speakers can be used effectively for sleep learning. The two most favored are a small speaker that can be hung from the headboard of your bed, and a speaker that can be placed under your pillow. The latter tends to be almost flat, so you can leave it under your pillow without creating an uncomfortable lump. Many of these speakers will have their own volume control independent of the tape player, making it even easier for you to select the best volume level for yourself.

Pillow speakers are available in most audio equipment stores. Because of variances in ohms and impedance, it is best to take your tape player along when shopping for your speaker. Let the salesperson select the correct speaker for your machine. This will help prevent a mismatch that may result in static or distortion. The importance of avoiding this type of interference was emphasized by A. W. Turnbow of the Sleep-Learning

Research Association in his monograph on the theory, application, and technique of sleep learning:

> "Mismatched impedance is a very common cause of failure in the sleep learning method. We have found that apparently even the slightest distortion of voice, hum, wow or flutter does not go undetected by the subconscious."

Automatic Timer

The final piece of equipment you will require is an automatic timing device. These are usually sold as timers to turn your house lights on and off while you are away, and can be purchased at most hardware stores or housewares departments. When selecting a timer, look for one that has four trippers. This will allow you the option of having two separate periods during the night in which your lesson will be played. Before buying a timer, check to see how noisy it is when the trippers turn it on and off. Some of these devices make a loud click that may disturb your sleep, so be sure the one you buy performs quietly.

For those unfamiliar with an automatic timer, it is simply an electric clock that is equipped with a series of pins to turn an internal switch on and off at preset times. You plug the timer into any outlet, set the clock face to the correct time, adjust the pins to turn the switch on and off at the desired times, and plug your tape player into the outlet usually located at the top or rear of the timer. At the set time, the timer will automatically turn the tape player on, allowing it to play until the time you selected for it to shut off.

With your timer set, the tape player plugged into

it, your lesson recorded on the endless loop tape, and your pillow speaker in place, you are ready to begin your sleep learning lesson.

How to Record Your Own Lessons

Now that you have assembled your equipment, you are ready to record your first lesson. Every detail about the recording is important and can influence the success or failure of the session; therefore, be certain to prepare the lesson with great care. As you record the lesson, be aware of the tone of your voice, the speed with which you speak, and the general attitude you convey through what you say and how you say it. Remember that the taped lesson will be received directly by your subconscious, where each nuance and tonal alteration will be detected and possibly interpreted.

From the work of numerous specialists, we know that sleeping people have a stronger response to the sound of their own voice than that of a stranger or friend. One authority proved that a person hearing his own voice in sleep is put in a state of high arousal, which provides a better reception to the recorded message. Although we do not know exactly why this is, it is clear that a sleeper responds more positively to the sound of his or her own voice, even to the content and characteristics of dreams. Use this to your advantage by *recording at least a portion of your lessons yourself*. It will also help your memorization of the material, because you will have first read it before engaging in sleep learning.

Another vital rule to follow when preparing lessons is to *use your own name*. Address yourself before, and even during, the lesson wherever possible. Sleep learning programs conducted at Oxford demonstrated that hearing your own name spoken while you sleep is an attention getter. Therefore, you should include direct address. An effective way to do this is to begin each lesson with the sentence: "Joe (use your name instead), you will learn and memorize everything you hear while you are asleep."

Before attempting to record the actual lesson, practice talking into the microphone. Reading a practice passage from an article or book will help you to judge the tone and emotional level of your voice. This will not only make you comfortable with the microphone, it will also provide the opportunity to determine the best sound level to use in the final recording. Some simple rules to follow when you are recording both the practice readings and the actual lessons are:

Speak slowly and distinctly. Your message, whether it is a lesson to be learned or a statement aimed at self-improvement, must be heard clearly to be understood. Unless you are using professional recording equipment, there is bound to be some loss and distortion. You can minimize its effect by speaking clearly and pronouncing each word carefully. Do not carry this to an extreme by speaking haltingly. Simply maintain a comfortable speed that does not interfere with the clarity of your words. Make certain there are no background sounds when you are recording.

Speak in a calm manner, using an even tone. If you develop "stage fright" when speaking into a microphone, practice recording your own voice until your self-confidence improves. It is important the lesson you are recording is received by your subconscious without any emotional tags, especially apprehension. You want your voice as well as your lesson to transmit complete self-confidence.

Be forceful. By this I do not mean that you should sound "pushy" or overly aggressive, which might provoke a negative reaction. Always keep in mind that the lessons you are recording constitute a set of positive instructions, and you want your subconscious to not only hear and understand them, but to follow those instructions.

Be brief and to the point. Simple, direct sentences are best. Do not allow your lessons to become too wordy by straying from the heart of the material. Try to stick to the basics of your lesson without adding extraneous material.

Each lesson should be no longer than twenty minutes. No matter what the subject, try to maintain a twenty-minute limit on each lesson. Within those twenty minutes, approximately ten should be devoted to the presentation of information. This means a twenty-minute lesson will contain two repetitions of the material to be learned. Longer lessons may result in too much information to be absorbed. Shorter lessons can be reinforced with additional positive affirmation statements such as, "You will remember this forever." As with other aspects of sleep learning, you must experiment with the length of lessons until you find the one that works best for you.

As you see by these guidelines, once you have acquired a thorough understanding of sleep learning, the basic instructions for its use are simple.

Using Prerecorded Tapes

There are many prerecorded tapes available today that are excellent for use with sleep learning. This is especially true of the subliminal tapes one can find in most bookstores. They cover a wide range of subjects, including languages, confidence building, and habit breaking.

If you decide to use one of these commercially produced tapes for sleep learning sessions, you may find it necessary to transcribe the information on the tapes and then record the lessons over in your own voice. Before doing so, try using the recorded tape first. Many of them are in a neutral voice and tone that will not have a negative influence on the success of your sleep learning.

Timing Lessons for Best Results

Now we come to the question of the proper time to present your lessons. When do we play the lessons for best results? Immediately after falling asleep? Just before awakening? In the middle of the night?

The experts have not been able to pinpoint a special time. There are sleep learning advocates who have selected certain time periods they believe are ideal for learning. Several researchers claim that learning can best take place during non-REM sleep periods, while others dispute this and say REM periods are best. Until this point is resolved, each sleep learner must begin by experimenting with the time schedule for his or her lessons.

Before going to sleep, you should listen to the lesson once or twice, then set the timer to replay it after you have fallen asleep. One technique is to set the timer to begin playing the lesson one half hour after you anticipate sleep. Set it to shut off the tape player for a two-hour period during the middle of the night, then leave it on until one half hour before you plan to awaken or before your alarm clock is set to go off. If possible, experiment with your ability to fall asleep while the lesson is playing and just let it run straight through.

It is impossible to estimate how many repetitions you will require to learn a given lesson. This can only be determined by measuring your success. The cases of sleep learning programs discussed throughout this book contain numerous examples of methods to test the results of sleep learning. Select the method that best suits the material you are learning and your own circumstances. Test yourself every few days until you can accurately estimate the number of repetitions you require for effective sleep learning. When you know this, you will be better able to develop your future sleep learning programs.

Earlier, I quoted Geoffrey Stocker of Britain's Sleep Learning Association when he likened sleep learners to scientists. As such, each of us must experiment with this method to find the techniques that answer our individual needs. The basic steps are simple, but the results depend on you.

When and How to Use a Conditioning Tape

Because of the various responses people have to the sleep learning experience, it is impossible to predict the level of success you will achieve from your first lessons. There is no way to determine in advance the need for conditioning yourself to sleep learning. Some fledgling sleep learners will have no problem with the process, while others may experience some difficulties, such as being unable to fall asleep or developing some anxiety about whether they will succeed. Any negative responses can be dealt with by conditioning yourself to make maximum use of sleep learning.

You will recall that the two English women who learned German through sleep learning were both presented with conditioning messages before beginning their actual language lessons. Miss Clark needed considerable preparation before beginning her lessons. In fact, it took several nights of sleeping in the Sleep Learning Association's dormitory with the conditioning tapes playing before she settled into a restful night's sleep. This was probably caused more by the strange environment than the anticipation of sleep learning.

It would obviously save time if you knew in advance

whether a conditioning message were required. Since this is not possible, you will need to experiment with this aspect of sleep learning to decide if you require this additional step. Two options are open to you. First, you can start by using a conditioning message without being concerned about whether you need one. This may prove to be the most efficient way. Second, you can forge ahead with your sleep learning lessons, disregarding the use of a conditioning message, using one only if the need for it becomes obvious.

Although it is possible for some people to learn while they sleep without the help of a conditioning message, as we have seen in previous chapters, it may be more productive for all sleep learners to make use of this method to help acclimate them to this new experience. One thing is certain: Using a conditioning or introductory message during the earlier stages of your sleep learning cannot hurt.

For those who do not want to get involved in a conditioning program, but wish to proceed directly into sleep learning, perhaps the simplest approach to resolving this issue is to preface your sleep learning lessons with a short direct command, such as, "You will remain asleep during the lesson, and will remember everything you hear while you are asleep."

This simple statement has a threefold value. First, it contributes to preparing you, while asleep, for the forthcoming lesson. It commands you not to awaken, and it instructs you to remember the information you will hear during the lesson. If this type of introduction is used, you should carefully monitor your results. If, after several weeks of lessons, you are dissatisfied with your progress, you will then want to add a comprehensive conditioning message to your program.

Should you decide to use a conditioning message, two options are open to you. You can purchase a professionally prepared and taped message, or you can record your own. Each has its benefits and drawbacks.

A prerecorded conditioning tape has the advantage of being professional, and is often prepared under the guidance of a psychologist or other authority. Such tapes are available from organizations that deal with sleep learning, such as the Sleep Learning Association in Britain and the Sleep-Learning Research Association of Olympia, Washington. You will also find conditioning tapes that are designed to enhance your ability to relax in your local bookstore in the section devoted to subliminal learning tapes.

A prerecorded conditioning message has two drawbacks. The first is cost. Some can run as high as twenty dollars for a single recording. Also, there is no way to evaluate these messages in terms of your individual need for conditioning. Since most are designed and recorded by people with experience in subliminal suggestion, we can assume they will be generally satisfactory.

Should you decide to forego the purchase of a conditioning tape, you will need to record your own. Provided you follow a few simple rules, there are several advantages to doing this. Two of these are that you will be hearing your own voice, and you will be able to address yourself by your own name. Both are highly beneficial to successful sleep learning.

It is important to use caution when recording your own conditioning message. This point cannot be overemphasized, since the goal of the message is to help you overcome "mental blocks," and to prepare you to receive the sleep learning lesson properly.

Before getting to the content of your conditioning message, we will discuss basic guidelines you should follow when recording your message. First, prepare the message in advance by writing a script. Read it several times to be sure you are comfortable with the statement. When recording, speak distinctly. The message will serve no purpose if you cannot understand it. Read it quietly but forcefully into the microphone. Keep in mind that you are giving yourself instructions you want followed. Maintain your voice on an even level, avoiding emotion or the sense of "barking an order." At the same time, do not allow your voice to become a monotone. A monotonous voice will sound boring and not provide the help for which the message is intended. "Barking an order" may awaken you, while monotony may be ignored.

The ideal length of your conditioning message cannot be determined with any certainty. Here again, the psychological makeup of each individual will have to decide the most effective length through trial and error. In some instances, it may be necessary to record a long message played for several nights before beginning your sleep learning lessons. Few people require such prolonged conditioning: however, you should be prepared to do so if it will contribute to successful sleep learning. For most, a short message of no more than five minutes will suffice.

A short conditioning message will allow you to use it every night for the first few weeks, or indefinitely if necessary. As we saw earlier, conditioning can only help the sleep learner realize the full potential of the experience, especially during the early phases.

Now, let us consider the actual content of the message. Here are several examples of conditioning statements. You may wish to include one of them in your conditioning message.

"You are asleep and relaxed. You can hear my voice, but will not wake up. You will remember these words forever."

"You will hear and understand what is said to you, and you will remain asleep. You will remember what you hear easily, and it will be available to you whenever you wish to repeat it."

"You will remain asleep, but will pay careful attention to the lesson that follows, and will remember everything you hear in that lesson. You will always be able to recall what you learn from this and all other lessons."

The above examples illustrate the essential thrust required of a conditioning message: Instruct the sleep learning student to hear the lesson, remember the material contained in the lesson, and not awaken while the lesson is being presented. A short conditioning message repeated two or three times before the start of a lesson, or presented by itself for several nights, should serve its purpose for most beginning sleep learners. As we discussed earlier, some sleep learners may need to use longer messages concentrating on a particular problem, such as awakening during or immediately following the presentation of a message, or some may require an increased number of repetitions of the lesson.

10

Using Sleep Learning Lessons

Whether you purchase prerecorded tapes prepared especially for sleep learning or tape your own recordings depends, of course, on personal preference. As we said earlier, the latter has the decided advantage of allowing you to hear your own voice and to address yourself by name, proven techniques that enhance sleep learning. On the other hand, using a prerecorded tape for learning a foreign language has the advantage of the correct pronunciation and accent of an instructor who is probably native to that language.

In this chapter, we will provide some examples of the type of material you should include if you decide to prepare your own lessons. These guidelines are for when you are recording your lessons.

To Learn a Foreign Language

The growing demand from both the private and public sectors for multi-lingual people has caused many colleges to reinstitute language requirements that had been abandoned during the 1960s. Language courses are also being embraced by high school students in increasing numbers. As travel and communications between different countries become increasingly easier, the requirement to converse in more than one language continues to expand.

International commerce leaves us no alternative except "learn to communicate or take your business elsewhere."

Sleep learning has been used successfully for years to teach languages. Many people feel it is the most obvious application of this teaching method. Here are a few tips that may help you when making your own foreign language lesson recordings.

The best way to learn a foreign language while you sleep is to combine a prerecorded lesson with some supportive material of your own. This blending of both techniques will help you learn faster and help you to learn to speak the new language more like a native.

Recorded lessons have become a boon to learning the conversational use of a foreign language. There are at least a half dozen manufacturers who sell foreign language lessons on long-playing records and cassette tapes. An advantage in using these recordings as the basis for your sleep learning lessons, instead of written lessons you can record yourself, is that the instructor on the recording will use the correct pronunciation and inflection, which becomes part of the lesson.

Once you have decided which language you want to learn, obtain a copy of the appropriate language record. The most economical approach is to use your local library. If your library has the facilities, play the record to screen it for scratches or background noises, such as a hum, that will interfere with your lessons. If the library does not have available the language you want to learn, you can purchase excellent language learning cassette tapes at most bookstores. Considering the heavy use library records get, purchasing a new tape is probably a good investment.

Using an endless loop tape, which you have presumably acquired, you can now prepare your first sleep learning lesson. Divide the prerecorded lesson into mini-lessons of a maximum of ten minutes in length.

If you accepted my earlier recommendation, your endless loop tape is twelve to fifteen minutes long. This means you will have two to five minutes of free time between each lesson. Put this time to good use.

The previous chapter contains instructions on how to use your own voice and name when preparing your lessons. Since we are using prerecorded material for the heart of your sleep learning lesson, the only time you can use your own voice and mention your own name is during the extra two to five minutes available on the endless loop tape.

Begin recording your lesson with a conditioning message that instructs you to pay attention to the lesson and to memorize it. Use the guidelines listed in the previous chapter to record a phrase similar to the following:

"Joe (use your name), you will listen carefully to the material you hear during this lesson. You will not awaken during the lesson. You will hear everything and memorize everything you hear while you remain asleep. Remember, you will not awaken, but you will remember everything in the lesson."

If time allows, repeat this instruction once or twice again.

Now, record the lesson itself. Most manufacturers of modern stereo equipment put a jack outlet for external speakers or recording devices at the rear of the phonograph or tape player. If your instrument has such an outlet, plug your tape recorder into it, set the volume at a moderate level, and start playing the prerecorded lesson. When the material for your lesson is about to begin, press "record" on your tape recorder. When the material for the lesson ends, press the "stop" button, disconnect the recorder from the player, and press the "play" button. Since this is an endless loop tape, there is no need to rewind it.

First, and most importantly, you will hear your own voice giving the instructions covered above. This should be followed by the lesson. Listen closely to the sound level to be sure it closely approximates the level of your own instructions. If it does not match, be sure to adjust the volume on the player and record the lesson again. Be careful not to record over your instructions. Also, listen closely for background noises that may interfere with your lesson or sleep. When you find the correct sound level, mark the volume control dial on the recorder so you will not have to search for it each time you record a lesson.

If your record player doesn't have a jack outlet through which you can record, you will have to hold the tape recorder microphone close to the stereo speaker to record your lesson. This is a less desirable way to record, since the sensitive microphone can pick up extraneous sounds. Some of this will be unavoidable, but if you turn off any clocks in the room, and other devices that produce even barely audible sounds, you can keep outside noises to a minimum. Even the hum of a refrigerator could cause interference.

You are now ready to begin your first sleep learning lesson. Carefully follow the instructions in the previous chapter for timing your lessons and the use of a conditioning tape.

When you are ready to record your next lesson, try not to record over the instructional message already on the tape. You can use this message for all your lessons, unless you feel a need or desire to change the wording as you progress. Thorough planning and careful preparation will contribute to your success at learning while you sleep.

To Break Bad Habits

The *Oxford American Dictionary* describes a habit as "a settled way of behaving, something done frequently and almost without thinking; something that is hard to give up. . . ." Although it is possible to have good habits, our main concern is with those habits that have a negative influence on our lives. Some of these become so fixed in our daily activities that they become too powerful for our conscious mind to control or change.

Some examples are fingernail biting, smoking, overeating, quick temper, and being unable to awaken on time.

If you have the desire and a strong motivation to overcome a bad habit, sleep learning will help, because it reaches into your subconscious where such habits normally find protection from external pressure on them. Achieving success in overcoming bad or destructive habits will depend on convincing yourself that you can and will stop the habit. This can be accomplished only through positive affirmations. Constant repetition of vital statements gives you the strength needed to break the habit that is harming your appearance, character, or personality.

When using sleep learning to conquer bad habits, deal with only one habit at a time. When you have mastered one, move on to the next. When preparing sleep learning messages aimed at stopping bad habits, your voice must be confident and reflect obvious control. You must point out the destructive aspect of the habit and stress the benefits of stopping. You may find the following is an example of a successful statement that you are free to use:

Nail Biting

> "My fingernails taste terribly bitter. My hands look ugly after I've bitten my nails. I will stop biting my nails. Gradually, day by day, I will become aware of now much better my hands look now that I've stopped biting my nails."

For Weight Reduction

Obesity, a critical condition that is often the precursor of heart disease or other serious medical problems, has created a tremendous industry that realizes hundreds of millions of dollars in profits annually. Thousands of books have been published, giving advice and diet plans for shedding pounds. Medical doctors and quacks pump out millions of "special" pills each year. Drugstore and supermarket shelves are weighted down with dozens of nonprescription drugs in the form of pills, powders, liquids, candies, and even tea for dieters. They're all aimed at one thing: weight reduction. With the limited exception of those individuals diagnosed with certain glandular problems, overeating is the cause of obesity.

We may tell ourselves that we are overweight because we do not eat the "right foods," or because we do not have time for "balanced meals," or because we do not "get enough exercise." While it is true that we should eat nutritious foods, the real problem is what we eat and the quantity of food eaten. If we are not getting enough exercise to keep the pounds off, obviously we must reduce our intake. If we are not eating balanced meals, we are probably operating on a feast to famine schedule or continuously stuffing ourselves with junk food that is high in calories and low in nutrition.

The problem most people have with overeating goes

deeper, though, and many times we treat the symptoms instead of the cause of obesity. Leslie M. LeCron, a clinical psychologist, identified this cause when he wrote:

> "In the development of obesity, the earliest cause for overeating goes back to infancy. When an infant is uncomfortable, it usually is hungry. Feeding brings comfort and the baby feels good again. Eating is then subconsciously associated with feeling good. The conditioning of the child is like Pavlov's dog. With the dog, the bell was associated with food. The infant associates food with feeling better."

How many times have we heard the expression, "Have something to eat, you'll feel better"? Unfortunately, we are so conditioned to feel better with food that we eat and do feel better. This reinforces the conditioning.

Sometimes the world around us seems to plot at increasing our problem. On television, in magazines and newspapers, and on billboards, sexy young (read slim) men and women are used to sell everything from bikinis to cars to fattening junk foods. On some level, we know most of these people struggle through life depriving themselves because their careers depend on their figures, and that beautiful slender girl really does not eat that candy bar she is holding to her lips. She is doing that just to convince us it is possible to eat candy and be slim. If she ate it, she would probably upset her caloric allowance and have to miss a meal or two. The advertisement upsets us, because if we eat that candy we gain weight. Why can't we eat it and be slim like her? This makes us feel bad, and what do we do to feel good? That's right, we eat.

There are, of course, other factors that contribute to our general weight problem. One may be our parents. If they were overweight during our childhood, we will have tended to adopt their eating habits, using them as role models. "If mom and dad are overweight, it's okay for me to be overweight." This belief is not necessarily something we are conscious of, but it is a message buried deep in our subconscious.

Let us take a look at the things we do to contribute to being overweight, and how sleep learning can help us deal with the subconscious causes that produce them.

1. We eat too much. We were told as children that it was important that we eat everything on our plates to grow big and strong.

2. We eat too fast. Even people who are not rushing off someplace appear to be in a hurry to finish their meal. This seems to be a uniquely American phenomenon. Europeans, who tend to be less burdened with weight problems, are generally slower eaters, sometimes taking several hours to get through one meal, while Americans almost always seem to be trying to set a record on how fast we can eat. If we slow down, the food will have more time to be digested, and our bodies will signal us to stop before we eat more. When we eat fast, the signal to stop reaches us after additional food has already been eaten and is on its way into our stomachs. The result is a feeling of being stuffed.

3. We eat to feel better (or worse). This is probably the most psychologically damaging reason for overeating. The satisfaction we get from eating is short-lived and eventually results in our feeling bad about overeating or the overweight condition it creates. (Some people eat to punish themselves. They want to make themselves look unattractive, because they believe themselves to be inferior or unworthy, and should look that way.) Then there is the depression cycle. We are de-

pressed about something, so we eat to feel better. Then we get depressed over having eaten so much, because it is contributing to our weight problem. This new depression eventually leads us to eat again and start the cycle over.

Since so much of the problem of being overweight seems to originate in our subconscious, it is logical that the subconscious must be treated as a cause, not a symptom of our eating habits. Through sleep learning, we can retrain our subconscious to send us different messages about food and its intake.

Naturally, sleep learning is not a complete substitute for developing your own willpower. This is not easy for most overweight people, since they probably would not be overweight if they had strong willpower. Let's be clear about one thing. Sending sleep learning messages to your subconscious aimed at weight reduction will help you to eat less and shed those extra pounds, but it is not going to work without some effort on your part. As you begin to see results from the nocturnal messages, you will begin to gain more confidence in your ability to control your own life, and build up your willpower.

When preparing your sleep messages, make a list of those things that bother you about being overweight. Is it your general appearance to others? Your own self-image? The difficulty you have in finding stylish clothing that fits? Your inability to keep up physically with your friends? Whatever the reason, and perhaps it is all these and more, that is where you want to concentrate your sleep learning messages.

Divide each sleep learning lesson into two sections. The first should discuss your goal, and the second how you will attain it. For example:

"When I lose thirty pounds, I will look so much better. Everyone will see how attractive I really am, and I will be more popular among the people I respect. To lose those thirty pounds, I will stop eating between meals, and eat less food at each meal. At home I will use smaller plates so the smaller portions will appear larger. When I finish a meal, I will be satisfied and not look for something to pick at afterwards.''

Change the message each week. Be sure you always emphasize the positive results you will get from losing weight, and the steps you will take to lose the weight. As you begin to see the results of your efforts, you will build more confidence in your willpower and, consequently, will gain increased control over your eating habits.

When you have reached your desired weight, change your sleep learning messages to emphasize what you must do to maintain that weight. Continue the sleep learning messages until you feel confident in your own ability to control your weight.

To Stop Smoking

Cigarette smoking is akin to overeating in that it is a habit that has an impact on your health and wellbeing. And, like overeating, it is a habit many people find almost impossible to break. It is possible to break the cigarette habit, and sleep learning can help you do it.

First, examine the reasons you smoke. The obvious ones are: it helps relieve tension, it gives you something to do with your hands, it's a social activity you share with others, it provides oral gratification. You already know some of the reasons you should quit: it's expensive, it's unhealthy, it's dirty, etc. Obviously these are not reason enough for today's smokers to quit, or they would be former smokers.

Most smokers realize they should quit, but their problem arises when they fail to translate that realization into a genuine desire to stop smoking. There is abundant information available from anti-smoking organizations on how to give up cigarettes, such as chewing gum instead of smoking. Avail yourself of this advice, then bolster your efforts with the aid of sleep learning. Many smokers fail in their attempts to quit because they program themselves for failure. They acknowledge beforehand that it is difficult to give up cigarettes and that they probably do not have the willpower to do it. This is where sleep learning can help.

Besides stating the benefits of being a nonsmoker, your nocturnal messages should also contribute to improving your willpower. Keep telling yourself that you are strong and can give up smoking. Get angry with your condition as a smoker and tell your subconscious that you are giving up smoking.

Here are some suggestions you will want to include in your sleep learning messages:

"Smoking is dirty, expensive, and harmful. I am going to give up smoking on (name a day). I will no longer have the urge to smoke.

"I'm no longer going to be a slave to cigarettes. Smoking will not rule my life anymore."

As you begin to see results, you can shift the emphasis of your messages. Tell your subconscious how good you feel after not smoking: "I no longer smoke and I don't need to smoke."

To Build Self-Confidence

Part of what we did in the earlier examples was to use sleep learning to build self-esteem. Many people lack the belief in their ability to act in their own best interests. Such people generally suffer from a low level of self-worth. A lack of self-confidence is usually indicative of this personality type.

Sleep learning can help build a better self-image through subliminal messages aimed at improving self-esteem. These can be simple basic messages, such as, "I can do that job," or, "I'm just as competent as anyone else."

You can begin building self-confidence by first convincing yourself of your ability and worth. The types of messages you use will depend on the particular problems you face. It might be best to start off with some generalized statements, such as:

"Tomorrow is a new day. I will start by showing the people I come in contact with how confident and self-assured I am, by being decisive and choosing what's best for me.

"I'm as good or better than most people. I am capable of doing as well as anyone else and even better."

Remember that self-confidence is a state of mind that is at least partially based on our own experiences. If those experiences have taught us to accept the inevitability of defeat, then we are programmed for defeat and are almost insuring it. The confident person already has one foot in the door of success. Sleep learning can help you hone that confidence by showing your subconscious the real value of your abilities.

11

Answers to Commonly Asked Questions About Sleep Learning

Is there a certain age when sleep learning works best?

No single age group will benefit from sleep learning more than another. Successful sleep learning does not depend on the learner's age, although it is possible that young children may have the same apparent advantage in sleep learning as they have in other forms of learning.

Does being susceptible to suggestion or hypnosis help your sleep learning?

Susceptibility to suggestion or hypnosis is most likely an aid to increased receptivity in sleep learning, but it is not necessary.

I have always been a poor sleeper. Are my chances of being awakened by sleep learning greater than a good sleeper?

Although being a good or bad sleeper may have some influence on your awakening threshold, whether you awaken due to the sleep learning lesson may be influenced more by other factors, such as the amount of sleep time you have accumulated and past experience with the stimulus of a recorded voice.

Will sleep learning affect the quality of my sleep?

We will let Geoffery Stocker of Britain's Sleep Learning Association answer this question. "Assurance can here be given that sleep learning does not adversely affect the health nor reduce the resting and restorative quality of sleep. There is ample evidence that sleeping patterns can actually be improved and also that students, following a hypnopaedic program of study, have seemed to require less sleep yet awakened 'more refreshed than usual.'"

What are my chances of using sleep learning successfully?

It is impossible to estimate an individual's expected rate of success before beginning sleep learning. Those who find the basic steps to sleep learning are not working for them will have to experiment with different techniques, such as altering the volume level or using shorter lessons, etc. Further scientific research combined with the accumulated experiences of widespread practical use of sleep learning will enable us to discover new and improved procedures to increase everyone's chances of success.

How fast can I expect to achieve results?

Some neophyte sleep learners begin to realize impressive results almost immediately, while others may take several sessions of sleep learning before they begin to see what it has accomplished. Sometimes the new sleep learner may require a period of conditioning, as we discussed earlier, before actual sleep learning takes place.

What would you say are the key elements to successful sleep learning?

Without a doubt, these are motivation, preparation, confidence, persistence, and repetition. To summarize what has been emphasized repeatedly throughout this book, motivation is perhaps the most important element in any type of learning. This is especially true with sleep learning. Without thoroughly preparing yourself for the sleep learning experience, you are reducing your chances of success. Confidence and persistence go hand in hand. The individuals who have confidence in their ability to use sleep learning successfully will be persistent in their efforts to do so. Repetition is a basic element that depends on your preparation of the lessons. If you prepare properly, then repetition comes automatically. Remember the first law of sleep learning as defined by Geoffrey Stocker:

**MOTIVATION + RELAXATION +
CONFIDENT EXPECTATION =
SUCCESSFUL SLEEP LEARNING**

Is it necessary to review the material to be included in a sleep learning lesson before going to sleep?

For most people, the answer is yes. Reviewing, or simply reading the material over before going to sleep, is actually a form of learning. As we saw earlier, learning just before sleep aids in recall. Even this small amount of learning will make the sleep learning lessons a reinforcement of what you have learned during the review.

Does sleep learning improve with practice?

Yes. At first the apprehension that can result from participating in sleep learning may interfere with real learning. With practice, we are better prepared for learning while asleep and will be more receptive to the lessons. Earlier, we reviewed a study by two researchers at the University of Florida. Although this project lasted only five nights, it contributed to our knowledge of improved learning ability with continued practice of sleep learning. During the first three nights, the average retention of the students involved was ten percent. During the final two nights, this improved to seventeen percent. If the study had continued, it follows that the retention rate would have continued to improve.

Are there certain foods or beverages that should not be used when one is sleep learning?

If you want sleep learning to be most effective, you must avoid the use of stimulants and depressants. This includes the consumption of alcohol and coffee. This does not mean coffee must be eliminated entirely. Each of us reacts differently to coffee. When using sleep learning, you should avoid drinking coffee in the late afternoon or evening. The effects of a cup or two of coffee in the morning will usually wear off before evening for most people. You should temper your intake of coffee and other stimulants to avoid hampering your sleep learning. Alcohol should be avoided entirely during a day that is to be followed by a night of sleep learning.

Will it help sleep learners who have a hard time falling asleep to take a sleeping pill first?

No. Studies of sleep learning in which subjects were given drugs to induce sleep inevitably ended in failure. Those who rely on drugs for sleep should make use of the relaxation/sleep inducing techniques discussed earlier, or relaxation tapes.

Although the cause is not presently known, drugs do

interfere with learning while asleep. This was vividly demonstrated in one sleep learning program, when the subject failed to learn anything while in a drug-induced sleep despite the fact she learned well during natural sleep.

Should the tape machine I use for sleep learning be placed close to the bed?

No. Although inaudible during the day, the sound of the machine operating has disturbed many people who were not awakened by the recorded message itself. Place the equipment as far away from your bed as possible to eliminate any potential disturbance.

Some Final Words

Now that you have a thorough understanding of how and why it works, you can begin successful sleep learning. Ahead of you lies a world of knowledge that might remain virtually untapped without your ability to use the third of your life spent in sleep. You can now turn that otherwise wasted time to practical productive use by learning a new language, committing important data to memory, building self-confidence, or any of the other marvelous things the practice of sleep learning can help you accomplish.

As a potential sleep learner, you are on the threshold of a new world where the horizons of personal knowledge are virtually limitless. I urge you to practice sleep learning just as you learned it in this book, and to share with others the enthusiasm you will feel as you begin to truly learn while you sleep.

If you have a sleep learning experience you would like to share with others, I urge you to write me at the publisher's address, which you will find at the front of this book.

I wish you many fruitful nights of restful sleep and effortless learning.

James P. Duffy

Appendix

Hypnopaedic Course in German

The Sleep Learning Association has kindly consented to the reproduction of the following portion of their course in the German language.

Guten Morgan.	Good Morning.
Wie geht es Ihnen?	How are you?
Und wie geht es Ihnen?	And you? How are you?
Sehr gut, danke.	Very well, thank you.
Ausgezeichnet.	Fine.
Ich fahre nach Deutschland.	I am going to Germany.
Auf Urlab.	For my summer holiday.
Sie haben Gluck.	Lucky you. (You are lucky.)
Es ist ein Wunderschones land.	It is a beautiful country.

Sie werden Ihren urlaub dort genießen.	You will enjoy your holiday.
Sprechen sie Deutsch?	Do you speak German?
Nur etwas.	Just a little.
Ich lerne Deutsch.	I am learning German.
Bis jetzt kahn ich noch nicht view.	I am not very good at the moment.
Deutsch ist eine interessante sprache.	German is an interesting language.
Es klingt auch sehr schon.	And it is a musical language.
Die Deutschen sind sher gastfreundlich.	The Germans are very friendly.
Ich habe Deutsches essen gern.	I like the German food.
Mir schmecken sauerkraut, wurstchen, und apfelstrudel.	Sauerkraut, sausages, and apple strudel.
Sprechen sie Englisch?	Do you speak English?
Ja.	Yes.
Wie heißen sie?	What is your name?
Ich heiße Herr Englisch.	My name is Mr. English.
Es freut mich sie kennenzulernen.	I am pleased to meet you.
Bitte setzen sie sich.	Please sit down.